D1384936

Frances Tenenbaum, Series Editor

HOUGHTON MIFFLIN COMPANY
Boston • New York 2000

Cooking from the Garden

Original and unusual recipes to enhance and preserve your garden harvest

MARGARET LEIBENSTEIN

Taylor's Guide and *Taylor's Weekend Gardening Guides* are registered trademarks of
Houghton Mifflin Company.

Library of Congress Cataloging-in-Publication Data

Leibenstein, Margaret.
Cooking from the garden / Margaret Leibenstein.
     p. cm. — (Taylor's weekend gardening guides)
  ISBN 0-395-88946-4
  1. Cookery (Vegetables). I. Series.
TX801.L45 2000
641.6'5—dc21   99-28991

Printed in the United States of America

WCT 10 9 8 7 6 5 4 3 2 1

Book design by Deborah Fillion
Cover photograph © by Rick Mastelli

ON THE COVER (clockwise from left):
Cassoulet (p. 86), Grilled Zucchini and Tomatoes (p. 75), Chris's Green Bread (p. 73),
Roasted Beets on Warm Spinach Salad (p. 12), and Sesame Sugar Snap Peas (p. 55).

CONTENTS

INTRODUCTION

Good cooks demand fresh, naturally ripened fruits and vegetables. They are aware that freshly picked produce, excellent wine, and olive oil of the highest quality can make the difference between mediocre dishes and extraordinary ones. They also know that however much they try to find fresh, unadulterated foods, they are limited by what is available in the shops around them. What is usually available are fruits and vegetables deliberately picked too early in the expectation that they will look ripe when the consumer purchases them. It is not surprising, then, to find that many great chefs are also avid gardeners who delight in the luxury of tomatoes that have real flavor and herbs that are fragrant enough to perfume their kitchens while waiting to be added to some superb dish decorated with fresh flowers.

Yes, flowers. Fortunately for those of us who rejoice in the beauty of flowers and delight in good food as well, it is no longer necessary to make a choice between one or the other. Gardeners no longer find it necessary to confine their garden plots exclusively to flowers or to vegetables. Some of today's most beautiful gardens display the lush leaves of multi-colored chard and rhubarb, of brightly colored chili peppers and the bell-like flowers of zucchini. Garden designs that were once limited to shrubs and flowers now make room for turnips and strawberries.

Gardener-cooks can, quite literally, have their flowers and eat them too. In a cook's garden, plantings of flowers are often divided between the purely decorative varieties and edible flowers such as nasturtiums, daylilies, calendulas, pansies, chives, and Johnny-jump-ups. Their petals and blossoms can be added to salads or used as garnish to brighten the food on our tables.

Clearly the bounty of today's garden can provide the table with both beauty and delicious, exciting meals. This book will help you do just that. I hope too that you will use these recipes to make delicious dishes at any time of the year, using produce from local markets.

Home gardeners and community gardeners have at least one thing in common. There comes a time every summer when you are forced to ask: "What am I going to do with all those _____?" After preparing the beds, planting, watering, fertilizing, and weeding, you have earned the right to enjoy the bounty of your labor.

A casual examination will show that *Cooking from the Garden* is organized specifically for the gardener—arranged not by the course (soups or desserts), but alphabetically by the vegetables ripening in your backyard. Some recipes are traditional, some are the result of the fusion of several cultures and traditions, all have been developed exclusively for this book, and all have been tested in home kitchens for taste and ease of preparation. Some recipes were contributed by chefs, restaurateurs, and food writers, specifically for garden vegetables. These recipes and those that I have developed are fine examples of the diversity and sophistication of modern American cuisine, which is characterized by its emphasis on fresh, garden-ripened fruits and vegetables.

With this book I hope to help you have fun, to "enjoy the fruits of your labor."

Bon appétit! ¡Buen provecho! Mangia bene! Guten essen! In any language, enjoy!

Chapter 1

Asparagus

It's the patient gardener who is rewarded by a crop of succulent asparagus. It grows in almost any climate, but a few spears will be ready for harvesting only after the second year. By the third year, however, they can be harvested lightly when they are three or four weeks old and will yield a more generous harvest in about six weeks.

Asparagus are one of the most prized delicacies from the garden. They were cultivated even in antiquity. The ancient Egyptians, Greeks, and Romans grew them, though not until the seventeenth century did mention of them appear in cookbooks.

In 1699 John Evelyn, the English diarist, author, and naturalist, described them in his important book, *Acetaria*. Evelyn wrote that asparagus were eaten raw with oil and vinegar and he recommended that they be "speedily boil'd, as not to lose the *verdure* and agreeable tenderness." This is still good advice.

Asparagus should be steamed or boiled only until they are barely tender and have turned emerald green. Serve them with a tart sauce, preferably with a lemon juice base, or use them in one of these recipes.

■ ASPARAGUS AND TOMATO MÉLANGE

2 tablespoons unsalted butter

1 teaspoon minced garlic

3 large golden or 6 medium red plum tomatoes (about 1½ pounds), peeled, seeded, and coarsely chopped

1 tablespoon mayonnaise

½ teaspoon freshly squeezed lemon juice

12–15 spears asparagus, ends trimmed and spears peeled and sliced into 2-inch-long pieces

1 teaspoon fresh minced oregano

Salt and freshly ground white pepper

I've always enjoyed this beautiful mélange of taste and color.

While the asparagus in your garden will be ready for harvesting in the spring, your supermarket produce section will have to provide the tomatoes. Yellow tomatoes are a bit less acidic and are preferable in this dish, but if they are not available ripe plum tomatoes are a good substitute.

In a small skillet, melt 1 tablespoon of the butter. Add garlic and sauté, stirring, until tender (do not allow to brown). Add the tomatoes and sauté, stirring, 3 minutes longer. Stir in the mayonnaise and lemon juice. Remove from the heat and set aside.

In a larger skillet melt the remaining 1 tablespoon butter. Add the asparagus and sauté over medium heat until just tender. Add the reserved tomatoes, sprinkle with oregano, and cook, stirring, about 3 to 4 minutes longer. Correct the seasoning with salt and white pepper and serve.

Serves 6

■ ASPARAGUS ITALIANO

In Italy white asparagus from Bassano are often prepared this way, though this dish is equally delicious with the fresh green spears from your garden.

Trim the asparagus spears by breaking off the root ends. Lay them flat in a large skillet for which you have a cover. Add 1 to 1½ cups water to cover the bottom of the skillet and bring quickly to a boil. Remove the pan from the heat and cover. Steam for 3 minutes or until the spears are bright green and just tender. Immerse them immediately in ice cold water to stop the cooking and drain them on paper towels.

Pass the hard-boiled egg yolks through a medium sieve and into a small glass or stainless-steel bowl. Stir in the lemon juice and mustard and, slowly, beating continuously, add the olive oil.

Chop the whites of the egg and stir into the lemon sauce. Add the anchovy and capers and taste. Correct the seasoning with salt and pepper to taste. Set aside.

To make the Red Pepper Coulis, heat the olive oil in a small saucepan. Add the garlic and sauté until soft. Do not allow it to color.

Discard the garlic, add the pepper-orange purée, pimentón, and kosher salt. Cook, stirring, over low heat until the mixture begins to bubble. Turn off the heat and stir in the sour cream or yogurt. Set aside.

To serve, arrange the asparagus spears in the center of 8 individual serving plates. Spoon a little of the coulis on either side of the spears and spoon the egg-lemon sauce over the asparagus.

Serves 8

1½ pounds asparagus, white or green

2 hard-boiled extra-large eggs, peeled, yolks and whites separated

2 tablespoons freshly squeezed lemon juice

½ teaspoon Dijon mustard

¼ cup extra-virgin olive oil

1 anchovy fillet, washed under running water, patted dry, and chopped fine

½ tablespoon capers, chopped

Salt and freshly ground black pepper

Red Pepper Coulis

1 tablespoon olive oil

1 clove garlic, smashed

2 roasted red bell peppers, peeled, seeded, and puréed with

2 tablespoons orange juice

1 teaspoon pimentón (Spanish smoked sweet pepper powder) or paprika

½ teaspoon kosher salt

1 tablespoon sour cream or plain yogurt

■ ASPARAGUS BRUSCHETTI

12 tips asparagus, each 3 inches long

$1/2$ teaspoon salt

5 cloves garlic

3 ripe medium tomatoes, peeled, seeded, and chopped

$3/4$ cup grated mozzarella cheese

2 tablespoons fresh oregano, minced fine, or 1 tablespoon dried

1 tablespoon capers, drained and chopped fine

12 $1/2$-inch-thick slices Italian bread cut at an angle

Freshly ground black pepper

Vinaigrette

2 teaspoons balsamic vinegar

$1/2$ teaspoon pomegranate juice or 1 teaspoon Reduced Balsamic Vinegar (see p. 110)

2 tablespoons extra-virgin olive oil

I tasted these crusty bread slices topped with garlic, tomato, and herbs for the first time in Rome shortly after World War II. Food was still hard to come by, but my Italian friends were determined to eat well even in the face of scarcities. To my delight they dug deep into their mothers' old Roman cookbooks and rediscovered bruschetti.

My version of this great Roman classic adds the delicate flavor and elegance of grilled asparagus tips. Since asparagus and tomatoes will not be ripe at the same time you will have to buy one or the other. If you must depend on supermarkets for your tomatoes, choose the pear or Roman variety.

I serve bruschetti as appetizers or as a light lunch with a tossed salad of young lettuce.

Place the asparagus tips in a small saucepan for which you have a cover. Add $1/2$ cup water and $1/4$ teaspoon of the salt. Cover and bring to a quick boil. Remove from heat, drain, and cover with cold water to stop the cooking. Drain again.

Cut the asparagus tips in half lengthwise and set aside on a paper towel to drain.

Mash the garlic cloves with the remaining salt until you have a paste.

In a small bowl, combine the garlic, tomatoes, cheese, oregano, capers, and pepper. Mound the mixture on the bread slices, place 2 asparagus tip halves on top, and place under the broiler until the cheese begins to melt and the tips begin to color.

To make the vinaigrette, whisk the vinegar and juice in a stainless-steel or glass bowl. Add the olive oil slowly, whisking constantly, until combined.

Sprinkle the bruschetti with the vinaigrette and serve.

Yields 12 slices to serve 6

Chapter 2
Beans

Snap beans, either the pole or bush variety, are one of the real rewards of a home gardener's efforts. Both kinds, whether they are green, purple, or yellow wax beans, will provide you with a fresh, crisp, and welcome early-summer harvest that you can consume immediately or freeze or pickle for future use.

These beans are probably the best known in the world. There is archaeological evidence that Mexicans and Peruvians cultivated them as early as 5000 B.C. Then Spanish and Portuguese explorers brought the seeds to Europe in the sixteenth century, and they were quickly adopted. It was not long before these legumes, now known variously as snap, string, or French beans, or haricots, became favorites in the Old World diet.

The recipes that follow are reminiscent of the origins of this delicious vegetable but are as contemporary as today's tastes.

■ FAST HARICOTS VERTS

5–6 cups (about 1½ pounds)
  haricots verts

5 teaspoons extra-virgin olive oil

1 teaspoon chopped fresh
  oregano or ¼ teaspoon dried

½ teaspoon kosher salt

Generous pinch of ground cumin

Freshly ground black pepper

1 large clove garlic, chopped fine

1 medium ripe tomato, peeled,
  seeded, and coarsely chopped

½ teaspoon balsamic vinegar

1 teaspoon fresh whole thyme
  leaves

Salt

Early summer is the time to harvest these versatile snap beans. They are best picked when the pod itself is firm and crisp and the seeds inside are very small or underdeveloped. Some beans are ready for harvesting while the plant is still producing blossoms.

In summer, Parisian street markets sport great mounds of these long, elegantly thin haricots verts, *which is French for "green beans."*

This dish is quick, low in fat, and a tasty accompaniment to meat and fish. It is also a delightful appetizer served cold on a bed of sautéed purple kale.

Snap off and discard the stems of the beans. Wash and pat dry.

Place the beans in a bowl, add 2 teaspoons of the oil, and toss to coat.

Sprinkle with oregano, kosher salt, cumin, and several grinds of pepper. Toss and set aside.

In a large cast-iron or heavy-bottomed skillet or sauté pan, heat the remaining 3 teaspoons oil. Add the garlic and sauté, stirring until tender. Do not let it burn. Add the tomato and vinegar and sauté, stirring, 10 seconds.

Add the beans and sauté, stirring until they are cooked but still crisp. Sprinkle with the thyme. Taste and correct the seasoning with salt and pepper.

Turn into a serving bowl or plate and serve.

Serves 6 to 8

■ STRING BEAN BATONS IN SAUCE

In America green beans are usually relegated to the role of side dish. Elsewhere in the world they are often served as the introduction to the main course. Though this recipe calls for a combination of yellow and green string beans, you can use any varieties you desire. String beans will be ready for harvesting in early summer, so mix as many varieties and colors as you have in your garden.

Snap the beans in two and set aside.

In a stainless-steel or glass bowl, combine the tomatoes and tomato paste. Stir in the vinegar and sugar and set aside.

In a heavy-bottomed saucepan large enough to hold all the vegetables and for which you have a cover, heat 4 tablespoons of the olive oil. Add the onion and garlic cloves and sauté, stirring occasionally, until the onion is golden.

Turn the beans into the saucepan and toss. Sprinkle with sea salt and sauté, stirring to coat, 4 minutes or until the beans' color begins to deepen. Stir in the tarragon and set aside.

In a stainless-steel or enameled saucepan, heat the remaining 2 tablespoons olive oil. Add the tomato sauce, correct the seasoning with salt and pepper and cook over medium heat, stirring occasionally to prevent burning, until the sauce thickens.

Pour the sauce over the beans, cover, and cook, until the beans begin to feel tender. Remove from heat, uncover, and let cool. Correct seasoning again if needed.

Serve, mounded, on a bed of radicchio if you wish, at room temperature.

Serves 6

1¼ pounds green and yellow string beans, ends trimmed

2 large very ripe tomatoes, peeled, seeded, and chopped coarsely

2 tablespoons good imported tomato paste

1 teaspoon balsamic vinegar

½ teaspoon granulated sugar

6 tablespoons extra-virgin olive oil

1 medium yellow onion, chopped fine

5 garlic cloves, smashed but unpeeled

Sea salt

2 teaspoons chopped fresh tarragon

Freshly ground black pepper

Radicchio leaves for garnish (optional)

CHAPTER 3
BEETS

Delicious beet roots are ready for harvesting when they are about 1½ inches in diameter, but they can be left in the ground one or two weeks longer without loss of sweetness. You can pick the young greens earlier, when they are 4 to 6 inches long, and add them to salads. They are, of course, the main ingredient in traditional Russian borscht, a beet-based soup eaten hot or cold; you can also roast or pickle them. To cook, cut the leaves level with the top of the beet. Trim the root. Put the beets in a small saucepan just large enough to hold them. Cover with water and bring to a boil. Lower the heat to medium and cook until just tender. Drain and run cold water over them to stop the cooking. The peel will now be easy to remove with a paring knife.

Another method is to trim, wash, and put the beets in a baking pan. Cover and bake at 300° to 325°F until tender, about 1 to 1½ hours.

The use of beets in the following recipes is anything but traditional, and I hope it will inspire you to include them in your garden plans.

■ BEETS WITH HORSERADISH VINAIGRETTE

Pickled beets have long been a favorite accompaniment to roasted meats, but their sweet and nutty flavor for its own sake has been neglected. This easy-to-make recipe blankets the beets in a sauce designed to bring out, not mask, their natural flavor.

You can cook and peel the beets early in the day, then slice and refrigerate them until you're ready to serve. They make an easy but elegant first course that has never failed to please my guests.

Trim the beets of stems, leaves, and roots. (Leaves and stems may be saved to make vegetable stock.) Wash and cook in boiling water to cover until tender. You should be able to pierce a beet to its core with a paring knife without much difficulty. Remove the beets from the water and submerge in cold water to cool. Peel and slice. Set aside.

Dice the onion fairly small.

To make the vinaigrette, in a stainless-steel, pottery, or glass bowl combine the vinegar and juice and stir to mix. While whisking, add the oil slowly until it is completely emulsified. Stir in the horseradish a teaspoon at a time to taste.

At serving time place 2 leaves of curly endive or kale on each of 6 chilled salad plates. Divide the beets among the plates and arrange them in an overlapping semicircle. Sprinkle with onions and drizzle with vinaigrette. Serve.

Serves 6

6 medium beets

½ Vidalia or Walla Walla onion, or other sweet onion

12 curly endive leaves or kale, washed, drained, and wrapped in paper towels

Horseradish Vinaigrette

2 tablespoons balsamic vinegar

2 teaspoons concentrated pomegranate juice or Reduced Balsamic Vinegar (see p. 110)

6 tablespoons extra-virgin olive oil

2–3 teaspoons prepared horseradish

■ ROASTED BEETS ON WARM SPINACH SALAD

4–6 golf-ball-sized beets

Olive oil

Salt and freshly ground pepper

Spicy Buttermilk Dressing

1 red onion, halved and sliced very thin lengthwise

¼ cup sherry vinegar

Juice of 1 lemon

Pinch of granulated sugar

Salt

1 tablespoon Dijon mustard

1 teaspoon or more Tabasco sauce

¾ cup grapeseed or canola oil

½ cup buttermilk

Freshly ground black pepper

2 pounds fresh young spinach from the garden or flat leaf from the store

4–6 ounces Roquefort cheese, crumbled

This dish was developed by Ana Sortun, the executive chef of Casablanca, a restaurant in Cambridge, Massachusetts. Ana is one of a group of young American chefs who are constantly surprising their diners with new and exciting ways of preparing native products. Like so many of her dishes it is simple and relies for its flavor on fresh ingredients.

Freshly pulled beets from your garden combined with freshly cut spinach will produce the desired results. If you have red and yellow beets growing in your garden, combine them for an even more festive dish.

And if you buy the spinach, try to get the flat leaves, not the old crinkled spinach that comes in a plastic bag.

Preheat the oven to 400°F.

Trim the ends of the beets and place them in a heavy baking dish. Drizzle with olive oil and season with salt and pepper. Roast for about 20 minutes or until tender. Let cool for about 10 minutes until you can handle the beets. Their skin should rub right off. Alternately, use a paring knife or peeler to remove it.

Cut in quarters and set aside. Reserve any oils or juices from the pan.

In a large stainless-steel or glass mixing bowl, let the red onion sit with the vinegar, lemon juice, sugar, and some salt for about 8 minutes. The onions will be lightly pickled and turn bright pink. Add the mustard and Tabasco and whisk. While whisking continually, slowly add the oil until completely emulsified. Stir in the buttermilk and add more salt and pepper to taste. Set aside.

Remove the stems from the spinach and wash. Spin dry in a salad spinner or place in a clean pillowcase, tie shut, and take it outside. Swing the pillowcase until the spinach is dry. Set aside.

To assemble the salad, divide the spinach among 4 dishes.
Set aside.

In a small sauté pan heat the beet quarters with a little
of their reserved roasting oils. When hot, add half of the
vinaigrette. Remove from the heat and divide the beets among
the plates. Season with salt and pepper and sprinkle with
cheese.

The spinach should wilt slightly and be a little warm
when eaten.

Serve immediately.

Serves 4

Chapter 4
Broccoli and Brussels Sprouts

Your first taste of broccoli and brussels sprouts may have been in your grade school cafeteria and therefore less than promising. But these nutritious vegetables can be a wonderful combination of crisp and tender if they are not overcooked. They have terrific textures and versatility for use in all kinds of cooking — steaming, roasting, sautéing. Both vegetables are from the same genus as the cabbage, *Brassica,* a strong indication of their depth of flavor.

Broccoli is rich in vitamins A and C, and medical researchers have recently found that it has cancer-preventing elements. It's a handy vegetable for those with little gardening space because the plants can be grown very close together.

The brussels sprout is a cool-weather plant with a harvesting schedule ranging from fall to early winter. And though it has only a small trace of vitamin A, it offers a hefty serving of vitamin C.

■ BROCCOLI WITH MUSSELS ON A BED OF ANGEL HAIR

The vegetable we eat is really a cluster of immature flowers. To be sure the broccoli has reached its peak of flavor, cut the stalks before the tiny yellow flowers begin to show.

In this recipe, so Mediterranean in flavor, I've combined the taste of fresh broccoli with the taste of the sea.

Clean the mussels, discarding any mussel with a broken shell or one that will not close when lightly tapped. Be sure to scrub the shells clean and rinse them quickly under cold running water. Do not soak them. Set aside.

Bring 4 quarts of salted water to a boil in a large pot.

In a separate heavy-bottomed pot for which you have a cover, heat the oil and add the garlic. Sauté the garlic, but do not let it brown. Just when it begins to color, remove it and reserve. Add the broccoli florets. Sauté, stirring, 2 minutes, or until just tender and deep green.

With a slotted spoon remove the broccoli and keep it warm.

Add the tomatoes and reserved garlic to the pot and cook, stirring, for 1 minute.

Add the mussels, wine, and pepper flakes. Stir, cover, and cook over medium heat, for 5 to 8 minutes, or until the mussels have opened completely. Add the broccoli and cook, stirring until heated through, about 1 minute.

Remove the pot from the heat and keep warm.

Add the angel hair pasta to the boiling water and follow the directions on the package. Do not overcook. The pasta should be *al dente*. Drain it thoroughly and turn it out onto a large serving platter.

Taste the broccoli and mussels and correct the seasoning with salt and black pepper. Spoon the broccoli and mussels over the pasta. Bring the remaining liquid in the pot to a boil and reduce slightly.

Spoon some of the liquid over everything and sprinkle with parsley.

Serves 4 to 6

1 pound mussels, scrubbed and beards removed

4 tablespoons extra-virgin olive oil

2 cloves garlic, peeled and slightly bruised or smashed

1 cup broccoli florets

2 medium ripe tomatoes, peeled and coarsely chopped

2 tablespoons dry white wine

1 teaspoon hot red pepper flakes

1 pound fresh angel hair pasta

Fresh Italian parsley, chopped coarsely for garnish

Salt and freshly ground black pepper

■ ROASTED BRUSSELS SPROUTS AND POTATOES

1 pound small brussels sprouts,
   halved

12 little red potatoes, scrubbed
   and halved

¼ cup extra-virgin olive oil

1 tablespoon chopped fresh
   rosemary or 1 teaspoon dried,
   mixed with

1 teaspoon sea salt

¼ teaspoon chopped fresh
   lavender blossoms or ⅛
   teaspoon dried (optional)

Freshly ground white pepper

Oven-roasted vegetables are wonderful with grilled fish. My favorite is this herbed combination of brussels sprouts and little red potatoes. They look lovely on the plate and are lovely on the palate.

Preheat the oven to 450°F.

In a medium saucepan, bring 2 quarts salted water to a rapid boil. Add the brussels sprouts and blanch for 3 minutes. With a slotted spoon, remove the brussels sprouts and drain.

Bring the water back to a boil and add the potatoes. Blanch them for 5 minutes. Drain and cool slightly.

Combine the brussels sprouts and potatoes in a shallow roasting pan. Drizzle with the oil and sprinkle with the rosemary, sea salt, and lavender blossoms. Toss to coat.

Roast until the potatoes are crisp and tender, about 25 minutes.

Grind white pepper over the vegetables to taste and serve.

Serves 6

CHAPTER 5
CABBAGE

Cabbages have become very popular in home gardens because, with a little planning, you can have a spring-planted crop and a second one for fall. They are attractive and decorative plants and, in addition, cooks will tell you that homegrown cabbages make for splendid eating, raw, pickled, or cooked in a variety of ways.

Germans ate "head cabbages," as we know them today, as early as the twelfth century. Several centuries later, it was discovered that sauerkraut, cooked and pickled cabbage, prevented scurvy. As late as the nineteenth century, British and American ships carried large barrels of sauerkraut for their crews. Today cabbage constitutes a basic vegetable in the cuisine of almost all countries.

St. Patrick's Day is synonymous with corned beef and cabbage in Irish communities around the world. In Korea, kimchee, a hot and spicy pickled cabbage, is central to the cuisine. The Chinese stir-fry cabbage, while in America no football tailgate party would be complete without coleslaw. No matter how you prepare it, cabbage is ubiquitous, tasty and rich in vitamins A, C, and K, a nutritional bonus for your efforts.

■ JAPANESE STUFFED CABBAGE

8 large cabbage leaves, preferably savoy

½ medium onion, chopped fine

½ carrot, scraped and chopped fine

1 pound lean boiled ham, ground or chopped fine

1 cup unseasoned bread crumbs

4 tablespoons unsalted butter at room temperature

1 egg

Pinch each of salt and black pepper

8 slices bacon

8 thin toothpicks

1 beef bouillon cube

5 tablespoons ketchup

1½ tablespoons cornstarch

Sweet-and-sour stuffed cabbage was a traditional dish handed down to me from my father, who got it from his mother, who got it from her mother, and so on. Imagine my surprise when, while dining in a friend's house in Kyoto, I was served the Japanese version of what I had come to believe was an exclusively Jewish dish.

Any variety of cabbage may be used, but if you have savoy cabbage growing in your garden it will make for a sweeter and more tender dish.

Shave the tough core of each cabbage leaf until it is flat and cook the leaves in boiling salted water until tender. Drain and dry on paper towels. Set aside.

In a stainless-steel bowl, combine the onion and carrot and mix. Add the ham, bread crumbs, 2 tablespoons of the butter, egg, and salt and pepper. Mix thoroughly.

Divide the filling into 8 balls. Place each ball on one cabbage leaf. Fold the bottom of the leaf over the ball, then fold each side over the ball, finally fold the top of the leaf down over the ball. Wrap one slice of bacon around the cabbage roll and secure with one toothpick.

In a sauté pan large enough to hold the cabbage rolls in a single layer, dissolve the bouillon cube in 2 cups boiling water, add the ketchup, and stir until completely combined. Add the rolls, lower the heat to medium, and simmer 20 minutes. With a slotted spoon remove the cabbage rolls to a warm serving plate.

In a small saucepan melt the remaining 2 tablespoons butter. Stirring, gradually add the cornstarch and mix thoroughly. Add 1 to 2 tablespoons of the beef broth and stir thoroughly. Be sure there are no lumps.

Lower the heat under the soup to low and add the cornstarch mix. Stir until the soup thickens. Cook a few minutes longer, stirring occasionally.

Spoon the sauce over the rolls and serve. Additional sauce may be passed separately.

Serves 4

■ BUBBLE AND SQUEAK STRUDEL

1 sheet frozen puff pastry, thawed for 20 minutes

1 russet potato, peeled

3 tablespoons unsalted butter

¼ cup grated onion, drained

½ pound lean ground pork

2 cups shredded green cabbage

1 tart apple, peeled, cored, and shredded

2 teaspoons fresh lemon thyme leaves

1 teaspoon kosher salt

½ teaspoon freshly ground black pepper

1 small egg, beaten

"Bubble and squeak" is the quaint name for a dish of cabbage, meat, and potatoes. Sometime around 1785 an English cook noticed that when potatoes were boiled, they bubbled, and when cabbage was fried, it squeaked.

Though bubble and squeak may have been christened in the eighteenth century, you'll find that it's as contemporay as today. Try it for lunch or a light dinner.

Preheat the oven to 350°F.

Roll out the pastry on a lightly floured board to a 15-by-13-inch rectangle. Place it on an ungreased baking sheet and set it aside in a cool place.

Quarter the potato and boil it in salted water until very tender. Drain and mash the potato. Set aside.

Melt 1 tablespoon of the butter in a large nonstick skillet. Add the onion and sauté, stirring, until opaque. Do not let it brown. Add the meat and brown, stirring. With a slotted spoon remove the onion and meat to a bowl and reserve.

Add the remaining 2 tablespoons butter to the skillet and melt. Add the cabbage and apple and sauté, stirring, until the cabbage is wilted and starting to brown. Add the potato to the skillet and mix thoroughly. Mix in the reserved meat. Sprinkle with thyme, salt, and pepper. Mix thoroughly.

Spread the bubble and squeak mixture lengthwise down the middle of the prepared dough. Brush the edges of the dough with some of the beaten egg and roll up, jelly roll–style, with seam side down, and turn the ends under. Brush the top of the strudel with the rest of the egg and make diagonal slits on the top about 2 inches apart.

Bake for 30 to 35 minutes. Allow to cool slightly and serve with a mixed salad.

Serves 6

CHAPTER 6
CARROTS

There is a variety of carrot that will grow in almost every type of soil and so more and more we find them in home gardens. Gardeners like them because they are usually ready for harvesting in two or three months, they can be left in the ground until needed without loss of flavor. The long, thin tapered varieties need to grow in loose soil with a good tilth, but the shorter, blunter varieties (which taste as good or even better) will succeed in less than ideal garden conditions.

■ GINGER CARROT SOUP

1 pound baby carrots or about
   6 or 7 young carrots, peeled
   and cut into 2-inch pieces

1 cup orange lentils

1¼ cups homemade or canned
   chicken broth

½ cup freshly squeezed orange
   juice

½ cup light coconut milk
   (available in Asian markets
   and many supermarkets)

2 tablespoons minced candied
   ginger

1 teaspoon granulated sugar

½ teaspoon kosher salt

¾ teaspoon garam masala
   (see p. 113)

1–2 teaspoons curry paste

Salt and freshly ground black
   pepper to taste

Sour cream for garnish

Fresh cilantro for garnish

Julienne strips of lemon rind cut
   into tiny cubes for garnish

In classical Greece, only the seeds and leaves of carrots and not the vegetable itself were considered fit to eat. Luckily we know better now. This sweet and aromatic root is one of the most versatile garden vegetables. It can be eaten raw in salads or out of hand. It makes frequent appearances steamed, glazed, stir-fried, or roasted, to accompany fish or meat. And it is even used in some favorite desserts.

Here's your chance to use your carrots in an enticing soup. This recipe calls for orange lentils, which cook more quickly than brown ones and will result in a lovely carrot-colored soup. And you can serve it to vegetarians by substituting vegetable broth for chicken.

In a 3-quart heavy-bottomed pan for which you have a cover, combine the first ten ingredients with 1 cup of water. Bring to a boil over medium-high heat, stirring occasionally. Lower the heat, cover, and simmer gently for 10 minutes or until carrots and lentils are tender but not mushy.

Remove from heat, taste, and correct the seasoning with salt and pepper.

With a slotted spoon, transfer the carrots and lentils to a blender jar or food processor fitted with a metal blade. Add half the liquid and process until the vegetables are puréed. If you prefer a crunchy soup, stop the processing before it becomes smooth.

Add the remaining liquid and pulse a few times to mix completely.

If cold soup is desired, chill several hours or overnight. Hot soup should be served immediately.

Garnish with a tablespoon of sour cream, a sprig of cilantro, and a sprinkle of lemon rind.

Serves 6

■ KATHY'S CARROT CAKE

Kathy Wheeler is one of my talented and creative assistants. In real life she is a devoted and treasured teacher of preschool children, but at one time she worked in the kitchen of a restaurant noted for its desserts. This cake, which is another way of using your homegrown or store-bought carrots, is Kathy's variation on a cake offered at that restaurant and one of her family's favorites.

With coffee in the morning, this simple moist cake makes for a sweet beginning. As dessert it is the perfect way to end a meal.

Place ¼ cup raisins in a small bowl and pour the juice over them. Set them aside to plump, 1 hour.

Preheat the oven to 325°F.

In a mixer or food processor, cream the butter with the sugar. Beat in the eggs.

Add the applesauce and yogurt and beat.

Combine the dry ingredients, including the walnuts and the remaining ¼ cup raisins. Add them to the applesauce mixture and stir until completely incorporated.

Fold in the plumped raisins with their liquid and the carrots.

Pour into a greased 9-by-5-by-3-inch loaf pan. Bake for 1 hour and 30 minutes or until the center springs back when touched. Cool in the pan on a rack for 15 minutes. Turn loaf out onto rack and cool completely.

Yields 8 1-inch slices

½ cup golden raisins

¼ cup apple juice or cider

1 stick (8 ounces) unsalted butter at room temperature

1 cup light brown sugar

2 large eggs

1 cup applesauce

½ cup full-fat or low-fat vanilla yogurt

2½ cups all-purpose flour

2 teaspoons baking soda

¼ teaspoon salt

1 teaspoon ground cinnamon

⅓ cup chopped walnuts

1 cup shredded carrots

Chapter 7
Corn

Of all the plants brought back to Europe from the New World by Christopher Columbus, corn is arguably the most important. Corn materials found in the Tehuacán Valley in Puebla, Mexico, tell us that corn was a staple in the diet of pre-Columbian peoples at least as far back as 5500 B.C. In the past Europeans used corn as a nutritious fodder for their animals. They ground it and used it in dishes like polenta in Italy and mamaliga in Romania. Today, however, even Europeans have succumbed to the wonderful flavor of fresh corn.

To prepare corn on the cob, cut the beards (the dark brown exposed silk at the end of the corn) off and trim the stems. To cook in the microwave: leave the husk on the corn and place it in the microwave on high for 2 to 3 minutes per cob. To steam: remove the husk and place the corn in a steamer basket over boiling water and steam, covered, for 5 to 7 minutes. To grill: steam or cook the corn on the cob in the microwave. Remove the husk and brush with oil or melted butter, then place the corn on a hot grill. Turn it periodically to prevent burning.

Most of the recipes that follow call for kernels of fresh corn. Since the sweetness of corn kernels begins to decline as soon as it is picked, you can achieve maximum taste by cooking it soon after picking.

■ FELIPA'S SWEET CORN SOUFFLÉS

In their youth my Mexican cousins were under the watchful eye of Felipa, their nurse, cook, and confidante. They are grown now, with families of their own, and a new generation is enjoying Felipa's lovely dish.

    Because the sugar in the supersweet corn varieties does not immediately turn into starch, it isn't necessary, as in years gone by, to harvest the cobs seconds before you plan to cook them. The flavor of these new varieties adds a very special kind of sweetness to these soufflés.

    Preheat the oven to 325°F.

    In the bowl of an electric mixer, cream the butter and cream cheese. Beat in the egg yolks. Add the corn and sugared milk and beat in.

    Sift together the flour, baking powder, and salt and add to the moist ingredients. With a wooden spoon, mix completely.

    Beat the egg whites until they hold soft peaks. Gently fold them into the corn mix.

    Butter 8 4-ounce soufflé cups or custard cups and fill them with the corn mix.

    Bake for 1 hour or until a toothpick inserted in the center of a soufflé comes out clean and the top is golden brown.

    Garnish with a spoonful of Pineapple-Pepper Guacamole (see p. 60).

    Serves 8

4 tablespoons unsalted butter at room temperature

1 3-ounce package of cream cheese

3 large eggs, separated

Kernels from 4 ears of corn

2 teaspoons granulated sugar dissolved in

1 5-ounce can evaporated milk

¼ cup plus 2 tablespoons all-purpose flour

1 teaspoon baking powder

½ teaspoon salt

■ SWEET CORN AND FRIED TOFU SALAD

6 large ears of corn

2 scallions, trimmed, white and 2 inches of the green, sliced very thin

1 small red bell pepper, roasted, peeled, seeded, and sliced in julienne strips

1/8 cup fennel sliced in julienne strips, blanched, and drained

1/4 cup chopped fresh mint leaves

1/4 cup chopped fresh flat-leaf parsley

2 teaspoons fresh sambal badjak, or to taste

Sea salt and freshly ground black pepper

1/2 cup canola or sunflower seed oil

2 cups firm tofu cut into 1-inch cubes

Lettuce leaves for garnish

The flavors of fresh-picked sweet corn and tofu contrast well with sambal badjak, the spicy Southeast Asian ripe chili paste in this salad. Sambal badjak can be purchased in supermarkets and Asian food shops.

Serve this salad with Cucumber Cooler (see p. 30), without the curry paste, and you have the perfect balance of hot and cool for a summer day.

Cut off and discard the beards from the ears of corn and leave them in their husks. Place them in the microwave oven and cook them on medium for 3 minutes, or put them in the top of a steamer and heat over boiling water for 3 minutes. (This process makes it easier to cut the kernels from the cob and keeps the kernels crisp.) Remove the husks and silk and, with a sharp knife, cut the kernels off the cobs. Discard the husks, silk, and cobs.

In a bowl, combine the corn, scallions, pepper strips, fennel, mint, and parsley. Toss to mix completely. Add the sambal badjak and toss to coat. Taste and add more chili paste if necessary. Taste again and correct seasoning with salt and pepper.

In a wok, heat the oil. It is hot enough for the tofu when a small piece of bread thrown in browns almost immediately. Remove the bread and add the tofu a few cubes at a time. Fry them until they begin to brown. Remove them to paper towels to drain and add more cubes. Continue this process until all the tofu is fried. Let cool.

To serve, add the tofu to the salad and toss lightly. Divide among 4 or 6 plates lined with crisp lettuce leaves.

Serves 4 as a main course, 6 as a side dish

CHAPTER 8
CUCUMBERS

In Mexico, when I was a child, vendors would sell peeled and halved cucumbers bathed in freshly squeezed lime juice and sprinkled with chili powder. I still remember the fragrant but astringent odor of the lime juice as I brought the cucumber to my mouth, then the cool moisture of the cucumber itself and the spicy chili finish in the back of my mouth. It was thrilling.

There are few things more satisfying for a gardener than the ease with which cucumbers can be grown, and nothing more refreshing than a ripe, succulent cucumber just picked from the vine.

■ Ma's Kosher Dills

2 tablespoons pickling
    spices

6 cloves garlic, unpeeled,
    lightly crushed

6–8 medium pickling
    cucumbers, or 10 small
    salad cucumbers

2 large dill heads

1 slice delicatessen rye
    bread, without caraway
    seeds

4 tablespoons kosher salt

My mother-in-law took inordinate time and care when preparing the traditional Jewish dishes she had learned from her mother in Russia, but she shrugged off compliments with the disclaimer "Maybe it's good, but not as good as in Russia." Only what she called her "kusher pickles" met her demanding standards.

"Why," I asked her, "do you think they're so good?" Grudgingly she allowed that "the pickles here [American cucumbers] are pretty good, like when I was a girl."

The secret of their unique taste was the delicious flavor of homegrown cucumbers, the absence of vinegar, and the addition of a slice of rye bread — which, combined with brine and spices, seemed to cause a kind of fermentation.

This recipe is a great way of preserving the extra cucumbers in your garden.

Pour boiling water to the top of a jar large enough to hold all the cucumbers you wish to pickle. Let sit 2 minutes, then carefully drain the jar.

Place 1 tablespoon of the pickling spices and 3 cloves of the garlic on the bottom of the jar. Arrange the cucumbers and dill heads inside and sprinkle them with the remaining spices and garlic.

Arrange the bread on top of the cucumbers. Try not to crumble it.

Dissolve the salt in 4 cups warm water and taste. If you prefer more salt, add it. If the mixture is too salty for your taste, add more warm water.

Pour the water, through the bread, right up to the top of the jar. Cover the jar loosely and set it aside in a warm place for 1 week.

Test the cucumbers for degree of pickling. If they are to your liking, remove the bread, cover the jar tightly, and refrigerate. If they require more pickling, cover loosely again and set aside. Check every few days.

■ SCANDINAVIAN CUCUMBER SALAD

Communities of Scandinavians around the world prepare this simple cucumber dish to remind them of home. It is traditionally served with grilled fish or roasted meats.

Using the thinnest slicing disk of a food processor or hand slicer, cut the peeled cucumbers into almost transparent slices.

In a stainless-steel or glass bowl, combine the cucumbers and onion rings and toss. In another stainless-steel or glass bowl, combine the sugar, vinegar, salt, and pepper with ⅓ cup warm water, and whisk until the sugar and salt are completely dissolved. Add the water to the vegetables. Toss, cover, and chill for several hours or overnight.

Serve in a chilled bowl and garnish with dill and chives.

Serves 2

4 young cucumbers, peeled

1 small onion, sliced very thin and separated into rings

⅓ cup granulated sugar

5 tablespoons white vinegar

½ teaspoon kosher salt

4 grinds black pepper

1 tablespoon each dill and chives, snipped with a scissors

■ CURRIED CUCUMBER COOLER

2 large or 4 small cucumbers

1 teaspoon kosher salt

1 tablespoon chopped fresh mint

Grated rind of 1/2 lemon

2 cups plain yogurt

Freshly squeezed juice of
    1/2 lemon

1/2 teaspoon curry paste

Cucumbers are very low in calories; if you are concerned about calories or fat in your diet, you can eliminate all the fat and reduce the calories from this recipe by substituting nonfat yogurt for full-fat. Nonfat yogurt is more acidic, so you may want to use less lemon juice.

If you plan to serve this cooler with Sweet Corn and Fried Tofu Salad (see p. 26), omit the curry paste.

This dish is better if you make it the day before, refrigerate it, and serve it chilled.

Peel, seed, and coarsely grate the cucumbers and turn them into a strainer. Sprinkle with salt and mix. Allow to drain 10 to 15 minutes.

Press as much liquid as possible out of the cucumbers and turn them into a medium-sized glass or stainless-steel bowl. Add the mint and lemon rind and stir to mix thoroughly.

Add the yogurt and fold it in gently until completely mixed.

Add the lemon juice a teaspoon at a time, stir gently, and add more juice to taste. Add the curry paste, mix, and taste. Add more curry paste if desired. Mix, chill, and serve.

Serves 8 generously

■ COLD CUCUMBER SOUP

*On a hot summer's day this refreshing cold soup, which needs
no cooking, served with a crusty bread and a salad of young
greens, makes the perfect light meal.*

*Weight-conscious cooks can substitute diet tonic water and
non- or low-fat yogurt for the regular tonic water and full-fat
yogurt. If you use low-fat yogurt, add only 1 tablespoon lemon
juice.*

Grate the cucumbers coarsely. Place them in strainer
and mix in the kosher salt. Set aside to drain 10 minutes.

Combine the yogurt, tonic water, water, lemon rind
and juice, chopped mint, and cumin. Stir to mix completely.
Add the drained cucumbers, taste, correct seasoning with
salt and pepper, and chill overnight if possible.

Spoon into 8 chilled bowls. Sprinkle with currants and
almonds and float a small mint leaf on each surface.

Serves 8 generously

4 medium pickling or other small
    cucumbers, peeled

1 teaspoon kosher salt

4 cups plain yogurt

2 cups tonic water

1 cup water

Rind of 1 lemon, grated

Juice of 1/2 lemon

2 tablespoons chopped fresh mint
    plus 8 whole leaves

1 teaspoon ground cumin

Salt and freshly ground black
    pepper

1/2 cup dried currants, plumped
    15 minutes in warm water
    and drained

1/4 cup toasted, slivered almonds

CHAPTER 9
EGGPLANT

The increasing popularity of eggplants has encouraged more and more gardeners to grow them. It was in India, where wild forms grow, that the eggplant was first cultivated, so it's not surprising that it plays such an important part in the Indian diet to this day. The Arabs, who use eggplants extensively in their cuisine, first introduced them to Spain in the eighth century A.D., and the Persians then took them to Africa. It's possible that African slaves brought the eggplant to Virginia in the late seventeenth and early eighteenth century along with okra, sesame seeds, and black-eyed peas.

These recipes represent the odyssey of this remarkable vegetable.

■ EGGPLANT, CHICKEN, AND BOW TIES

1 boned and skinned chicken breast, cut into thin strips

½ cup Zesty Lemon Dressing (see p. 80)

2 small 3–5-inch eggplants or 1 large

Olive oil for brushing eggplant

10 ounces medium-sized bow tie pasta

1 small chili pepper, such as Tabasco or jalapeño

2 tablespoons extra-virgin olive oil

1 clove garlic, crushed

½ cup radishes, sliced thin

3 ounces fresh broccoli, broken into tiny florets, blanched, and drained

2 tablespoons chopped fresh parsley

1 tablespoon chopped fresh tarragon

½ teaspoon kosher salt

¼ teaspoon freshly ground black pepper

In the south of Italy pasta is most often flavored with tomatoes. Much as I love tomatoes, after many months of living in Rome, I was ready to try something new. So you can imagine my delight when a Neapolitan friend served me a dish of pasta and eggplant roasted over a wood fire.

We dined on a sunny terrace overlooking the Mediterranean, handsomely decorated with large terra-cotta pots in which eggplants of varying shapes, sizes, and colors grew glittering in the sun like living Christmas tree ornaments.

You will have to find your own terrace, but this combination of marinated chicken, eggplant, other garden-fresh vegetables, and pasta will go a long way toward duplicating that wonderful experience in Naples long ago.

If you pick the eggplants from your own garden, harvest them when they are between four and five inches long and have shiny skins. If you buy them in a market, pick the smaller, shiny specimens. Dull skin indicates that the eggplant has either been picked too late or has spent too much time on the market shelf.

Preheat the oven to 400°F or fire up the grill.

In a small stainless-steel or glass bowl, combine the chicken and Zesty Lemon Dressing. Set aside.

Prick the eggplant all over with a fork, brush with oil, and bake it in a roasting pan for 30 minutes or until it collapses and is cooked through. Or grill the eggplant but do not prick it or brush it with oil. Set the eggplant aside.

Cook the pasta in salted water until *al dente*, drain, and keep warm.

Cut the eggplant in half and scoop out the flesh. Discard the shell and mash or put the flesh in the bowl of a food processor fitted with a metal blade and purée. Set aside.

Wearing rubber gloves, remove the stem from the chili pepper, cut it lengthwise, and remove and discard the seeds. Remove the gloves when you are through handling the pepper.

In a large nonstick skillet heat the 2 tablespoons oil and add the garlic and chili pepper. Cook, stirring, until the garlic begins to brown. Discard both the garlic and chili and add the radishes and broccoli and cook, stirring, 30 seconds. Remove the skillet from the heat and with a slotted spoon transfer the vegetables to a bowl. Keep warm.

Return the skillet to the stove and add a little oil if necessary. Drain the chicken and add it to the skillet. Cook, stirring constantly, until the meat begins to brown. Stir in the eggplant, sprinkle with the parsley and tarragon, and cook, stirring, 3 minutes.

Transfer the warm pasta to a serving bowl, turn the hot eggplant onto the pasta, and toss. Sprinkle with the hot radishes, broccoli, salt, and pepper, and toss lightly again. Correct seasoning.

Serve immediately.

Serves 6

■ BERENJENA DELEITABLE (Delectable Eggplant)

2 4- or 5-inch eggplants or 1 large

Olive oil, if you plan to grill the
    eggplant

2 small onions

¼ cup chopped chives

2 pickled jalapeño peppers

1 clove garlic, sliced

¾ cup mayonnaise

1 teaspoon lime juice

½ teaspoon Maggi Seasoning or
    Worcestershire sauce

½ cup heavy cream

1 teaspoon concentrated
    pomegranate juice or Reduced
    Balsamic Vinegar (see p. 110)

Salt and freshly ground black
    pepper

From baba ghanoush in the Middle East to mock caviar on crackers in California, eggplant dips and spreads have always delighted diners. If you roast the eggplant over charcoals, the dish will have a subtle smoky flavor.

Preheat the oven to 400°F or fire up the barbecue.

Prick the eggplant all over with a fork. Place it in a roasting pan, brush it with olive oil, and bake 30 minutes or until the eggplant collapses and is very soft. If you plan to roast the eggplant over hot coals, do not prick it or brush it with oil. Place it on the grill over glowing coals. Roast it, turning it from time to time, until the eggplant collapses and is very soft.

Allow it to cool enough to handle. Peel and transfer the pulp to the bowl of a food processor fitted with a metal blade.

Add the onions, chives, jalapeño, and garlic, and process 2 minutes or until quite smooth. Add the mayonnaise, lime juice, and Maggi or Worcestershire and pulse until blended.

Transfer the eggplant mixture to a bowl and whisk in the cream a little at a time until fully incorporated. Mix in the pomegranate juice.

Taste and correct the seasoning with salt and pepper.

Serve as a dip or as a spread on crackers. Berenjena Deleitable is also delicious on sliced ripe tomatoes or cold grilled fish or chicken.

Yields 4 cups

■ SPICY STIR-FRIED EGGPLANT

Nina Simonds is one of America's leading experts on the food of China. Though trained in Paris at La Varenne, she lived for many years in Taiwan, studying the Mandarin language and Chinese cuisine. Her lectures, articles, and books on Chinese cooking are the happy results of her acquired expertise.

She depends heavily on the use of fresh vegetables, either alone or in combination with meat, poultry, or fish. She has taught us that quick stir-frying seals in the remarkable flavors of ripe garden products.

I think you'll find Nina's eggplant stir-fry as delicious and easy to prepare as I did.

Preheat the oven to 450°F.

Rinse the eggplant, cut off the stems, and cut the eggplant in half lengthwise. Cut each half twice more lengthwise so that each piece is about 3 inches long and 1 inch wide. (You now have 12 lengths.) If using ordinary eggplant, peel the eggplant, cut off the stem, and cut into 3-inch lengths. Arrange the eggplant on cookie sheets that have been lightly greased. Bake for 15 minutes, turning once.

Lightly chop the ground turkey until fluffy and place it in a bowl. Add soy sauce and sesame oil, and toss lightly. Combine the Minced Seasonings ingredients and set aside and combine the Spicy Sauce ingredients and set aside.

Heat a wok or a skillet, add the 1½ tablespoons corn oil, and heat. Add the Minced Seasonings and the turkey. Stir-fry until fragrant, about 15 seconds. Add the Spicy Sauce and the eggplant. Toss lightly to coat. Once the eggplant has absorbed the sauce, and the meat is thoroughly cooked, transfer them to a platter and serve.

Serves 6 to 8

1½ pounds Chinese or Japanese eggplant or any other small eggplant

½ pound ground turkey

1½ tablespoons soy sauce

1 teaspoon sesame oil

Minced Seasonings

2 tablespoons minced garlic

2 tablespoons scallions, white only, minced

1½ tablespoons fresh gingerroot, peeled and minced

1 teaspoon hot chili paste (available in Asian markets or supermarkets)

Spicy Sauce

3½ tablespoons soy sauce

2 tablespoons granulated sugar

3 tablespoons Chinese black vinegar or

1½ tablespoons Worcestershire sauce

1 teaspoon sesame oil

2 tablespoons safflower or corn oil

2 tablespoons Chinese rice wine or Japanese sake

1½ tablespoons corn oil

CHAPTER 10
LEAFY GREENS
Lettuce, Spinach, Arugula, Chard, Kale, and Sorrel

Today's salads combine many lettuce varieties and leafy greens. A working kitchen garden may have a mix of lettuces, spinach, arugula, sorrel, chards, and other such vegetables that can be picked fresh on the day they're needed.

Lettuce varieties fall into three categories; crisphead like iceberg; butterheads like Boston or romaine; and looseleaf like salad bowl or oak leaf. All are best harvested early in the morning when they are their crispest. And it is best to pick only the amount you plan to eat that day, place the leaves in a loosely fastened plastic bag and put the bag in the refrigerator until needed.

Decorative additions to any garden are the new ruby and yellow varieties of chard. They are delicious and equally beautiful when cooked.

In the garden, chard, whether white, ruby, or yellow, will produce two harvests per growing season. If the entire top of the plant is harvested about 2 inches above the level of the soil when the leaves are about a foot tall, tender leaves will soon begin to grow and will eventually give you a second harvest.

■ REFRESHING BABY LETTUCE SALAD

Summertime is truly salad time, so enjoy. You can always buy a mixture of "mesclun" looseleaf lettuces in most supermarkets these days, but the lettuces you pick just before serving are sweeter.

The gardener now has enough varieties of looseleaf lettuce to guarantee interesting summertime fare. Looseleaf lettuces do not produce heads, so be sure to pick the larger outer leaves often to encourage new and tender growth. This zesty salad will be a delightful reward for your efforts.

Mash the garlic and salt together into a paste. In a nonreactive bowl combine the garlic paste, lemon juice, 1 teaspoon cold water, lemon rind, and sugar. Whisk until the sugar is dissolved. Continue to whisk and add the oil slowly until combined well. Taste and add salt and pepper.

Combine the salad ingredients in a serving bowl. Whisk the dressing to combine. Add half the dressing, toss, and taste. Add the remaining dressing to taste.

Serves 4 to 6

Dressing

1 clove garlic, minced

1/8 teaspoon salt

1 tablespoon freshly squeezed lemon juice

1/4 teaspoon grated lemon rind

1/4 teaspoon granulated sugar

3 tablespoons extra-virgin olive oil

Salt and freshly ground black pepper

Salad

4–6 cups mixed baby lettuce leaves, washed and spun dry

1/4 cup thinly sliced radish rounds

1/2 cup coarsely grated carrots

1 tablespoon julienne strips of fresh mint leaves

1/8 cup pitted, thinly sliced kalamata or niçoise olives (optional)

■ CAESAR'S PENNE

1 pound penne pasta

3–4 tablespoons commercial Caesar salad dressing

1 cup baby spinach, torn in small pieces

5 basil leaves, snipped into small pieces with scissors

¼ cup freshly grated Parmesan cheese

This is the perfect dish for those days when you are too busy to shop and are too tired to cook, those times when you'd planned to settle for a peanut butter sandwich, but friends drop in expecting to be fed.

A few snips of basil and young spinach leaves pinched fresh from your garden are all that you need to make this pasta a very special treat.

Cook the pasta in a large pot of salted water until *al dente*. Drain it well and turn it into a serving bowl.

Add the dressing and toss. Taste and add more if necessary.

Add the spinach and basil and toss. The heat of the pasta will tend to slightly wilt the vegetables.

Sprinkle with the cheese, toss, and serve.

Pass additional cheese if desired.

Serves 6

■ WALNUT AND ARUGULA SALAD

Arugula is a quick-growing green that is a welcome addition to the kitchen garden. It is easy to grow and, when not consumed by gourmet rabbits or raccoons, can be harvested all summer long. It is a favorite with container gardeners because it will flourish on any sunny deck or windowsill. In the garden it's best to plant seeds every few weeks for a summer supply of tender leaves.

Because of its somewhat peppery, tangy flavor, arugula, which is sometimes called rocket salad, or roquette *in France, is a tasty addition to simple mixed-lettuce salads. Here it's used as the principal ingredient with great success.*

4 cups arugula

1½ tablespoons sherry vinegar or a good white wine vinegar

1 teaspoon Dijon mustard

¼ teaspoon granulated sugar

5 grinds of black pepper

Salt

⅓ cup extra-virgin olive oil

½ cup walnuts, chopped small and lightly toasted

⅓ cup dried currants

Trim the arugula stems, rinse, and spin the leaves dry. Wrap them in layers of paper towel, place in a plastic bag, and set aside in the refrigerator.

In a small stainless-steel or glass bowl, whisk together the vinegar, mustard, sugar, and pepper. Add salt to taste.

Continue whisking while adding the oil in a slow stream.

At serving time, tear the arugula leaves in half, combine them with the dressing to taste, and toss. Reserve any leftover dressing for another time.

Divide the salad among 6 chilled serving plates and sprinkle each with the walnuts and currants.

Serves 6

▪ SWISS CHARD AND MUSCOVY DUCK

4 boned Muscovy duck breasts

½ cup red wine

9 tablespoons soy sauce

2 small onions, peeled and
    quartered

½ teaspoon kosher salt

8 scallions, trimmed, white and
    2 inches of green

1 tablespoon dark brown sugar

1 teaspoon ground cinnamon

1½ pounds red and yellow Swiss
    chard, stems trimmed, washed
    thoroughly

4 tablespoons Spanish extra-virgin
    olive oil

1 cup chopped red onion

3 tablespoons pine nuts

3 tablespoons golden raisins,
    soaked in

½ cup cream sherry for about
    15 minutes

1 tablespoon orange juice

Salt and freshly ground black
    pepper

Edible flowers such as
    nasturtiums, marigolds,
    Johnny-jump-ups, violets, or
    rose petals for garnish
    (optional)

The combination of Swiss chard and roasted duck breast makes this an exceptional company dish. Duck breasts can be purchased in many supermarkets, frozen and vacuum-wrapped. If you're lucky enough to know your market's butcher, he can order them for you.

This beautiful dish is easier than it looks because the duck is cooked for 8 minutes the day before, then roasted for a mere 24 minutes before serving.

The day before you plan to serve the duck, pierce the breast skins all over with a fork.

In a pot just large enough to hold the breasts, combine 3 cups water, wine, 6 tablespoons of the soy sauce, onions, kosher salt, and scallions, and mix. Place the breasts, skin side up, in the pot and bring rapidly to a boil. Cover and boil for 4 minutes. Turn the breasts over and cover the pot again. Boil for an additional 4 minutes.

Remove the pot from the heat, cool, and refrigerate overnight.

The next morning scrape the fat that has formed on the surface and discard. Return the duck to the refrigerator. Preheat the oven to 450°F. Two hours before cooking, remove the duck in its marinade from the refrigerator and allow it to come to room temperature.

Make the basting sauce: in a small bowl, combine the remaining 3 tablespoons soy sauce, the sugar and cinnamon, and whisk until the sugar has completely dissolved and the cinnamon is incorporated. Set aside.

To roast, remove the breasts from their marinade and place them on a rack in a shallow roasting pan. Discard the marinade.

Baste the duck all over with the basting sauce and place it, skin side up, on a rack. Roast 7 minutes. Baste the breasts all over again and turn them skin side down. Roast for an additional 7 minutes. Baste the breasts all over for the third time and turn skin side up. Roast for 7 additional minutes. Pierce the breasts with a fork. If the juices run slightly pink, it is done. This method results in slightly rare meat. If you prefer your meat more well done, increase the roasting time by 2 minutes for each side.

Remove the breasts from the oven and let stand in a warm place.

Cut the Swiss chard across the leaves into 2- to 3-inch strips. Set aside.

In a large skillet for which you have a cover, heat the oil. Add the red onion and pine nuts, and stir. Drain the raisins, reserve 1 tablespoon sherry, and add the raisins to the skillet.

When the pine nuts begin to color and the onions are soft, add the reserved sherry and orange juice. Deglaze the skillet, scraping anything that has stuck to the pan. Add the Swiss chard, toss, and cover. Lower the heat and cook 5 to 8 minutes or until the leaves are wilted and stems are tender.

Taste and season with salt and freshly ground black pepper to taste.

With a very sharp knife, slice the duck breasts about a ½ inch wide across, keeping the slices in place. Set aside.

On a warm serving platter, pile the vegetables in the center. Place the sliced breasts around the vegetables. Pour any meat juices on the vegetables and garnish with edible flowers.

Serves 6

■ CHARD AND BAKED SALMON

1½ pounds salmon fillet

Juice of ½ lemon

½ cup sour cream

3 tablespoons mayonnaise

1 large ripe tomato, peeled, seeded, and chopped

2 medium portobello mushroom caps, brushed clean and chopped fine

3 tablespoons chopped fresh chives

2 tablespoons chopped fresh flat-leaf parsley

1 tablespoon chopped fresh tarragon

Salt and freshly ground white pepper

6–10 leaves Swiss chard, washed, spun dry, and stems trimmed

6–10 leaves sorrel, washed and spun dry

3 tablespoons unsalted butter

Salt and freshly ground black pepper

Tiny diamonds cut from red and yellow bell peppers as garnish (optional)

Lemon wedges as garnish (optional)

Swiss chard and sorrel are greens that were too long ignored by home gardeners. Luckily that is no longer true. Chard grows well in both warm and cool temperatures and makes a decorative addition to any garden. It is the sautéed combination of the chard and sorrel that makes this beautiful dish so distinctive.

Salmon farming has made this once scarce fish available year-round. Combined with fresh tomatoes, and herbs freshly picked from the garden and served on a bed of sliced chard and sorrel, the salmon becomes a gustatory experience.

Serve it with plain boiled and buttered potatoes.

Preheat the oven to 400°F.

Butter a shallow baking dish large enough to hold the salmon. Sprinkle the fish with the lemon juice and place in the baking dish.

Combine the sour cream and the mayonnaise. Stir in the tomato, mushroom caps, and herbs, and mix. Correct the seasoning with salt and white pepper to taste.

Spread the mix over the salmon, and bake 15 to 17 minutes, or more if necessary, depending on the thickness. Insert a toothpick at the thickest part. If it slips in easily, the fish is done. Do not bake too long, for if the fish flakes, it is overcooked.

While the fish is baking, sauté the chard and sorrel in the butter for 5 minutes or until the greens are cooked. Season with salt and black pepper to taste and arrange on a serving platter. Place the fish on top of the vegetables and sprinkle with the colored bell pepper garnish, if desired. Lemon wedges are an optional accompaniment. Serve.

Serves 4 to 6

■ CURLY KALE SAUTÉ

If you want to add vitamin C to your diet there is, perhaps, no better food to eat than kale. One cup of cooked kale provides the equivalent of the vitamin C in one cup of orange juice. It also contains significant quantities of vitamin A and many essential minerals.

Kale makes an excellent decorative plant in any garden because it is very hardy, has a full curly head, and can tolerate early frosts. It provides a long supply of the tasty leaves because harvesting can begin when leaves are only five or six inches long. And you can use even smaller, more tender leaves in salads.

4 slices sugar-cured bacon

1 clove garlic, minced

1 small onion, chopped fine

4 cups packed coarsely chopped kale, washed, drained, and tough stems removed

1 teaspoon fresh lime juice

Salt and freshly ground black pepper

In a large nonstick skillet over medium-low heat, render the bacon until it begins to crisp.

Add the garlic and onion. Cook, stirring, 1 minute. Add the kale and toss to coat. Cook, stirring, until the kale is a deep emerald green and tender. Turn into a warm serving dish. Add the lime juice and toss. Taste and season with salt and pepper. Serve immediately.

Serves 6

■ SORREL SOUP

2 cups homemade or canned clear chicken broth

2 cups coarsely chopped, washed, and dried sorrel leaves, stems trimmed

4 jumbo egg yolks

3 tablespoons lemon juice

Grated rind of 1/2 lemon

1 cup whole buttermilk

Pinch each of nutmeg, white pepper, and cayenne

Salt and freshly ground black pepper

Fresh chervil or cilantro for garnish (optional)

More and more gardeners are adding sorrel to their herb gardens because it is so easy to grow and is so versatile. In Europe, it grows wild and is used in a multitude of traditional family recipes. This version of the Russian summer soup, schav, *will make perfect use of this "new" herb in the garden.*

Bring broth to a boil and add sorrel. Reduce the heat to low and simmer until the greens are tender, about 7 minutes.

With a slotted spoon, remove the greens and place them in a blender or in a food processor fitted with a steel blade. Add 3/4 cup broth and process until the greens are puréed. Combine the liquefied greens with the remaining broth and bring back to simmer.

In a stainless-steel or glass bowl, beat the egg yolks with the lemon juice. Add the lemon rind, buttermilk, and the spices, and stir to mix completely.

Add 1/2 cup hot soup into the egg mixture, stirring constantly. Continue to stir and add the warmed egg mixture slowly into the broth. Continue stirring over low heat until the soup begins to thicken slightly. Do not let the soup boil.

Remove the pan from the heat and set in a bowl filled with cracked ice. Correct the seasoning with salt and black pepper. Stir until the soup is cool. Pour into a chilled tureen or bowl and refrigerate.

Serve in 6 chilled bowls. To garnish, float chervil or cilantro leaves.

Serves 6

Chapter 11
Onions, Leeks, and Garlic

Onions, leeks, and garlic are the most basic and versatile of all vegetables. They are eaten raw, fried, boiled, and roasted. You find them in soups, stews, pickles, and chutneys. Onions are so important in the Indian diet that a recent slight rise in their price caused riots and political demonstrations. And they are so much a part of American cooking that it is hard to believe that they haven't always grown here. Onions became popular in Europe only in the Middle Ages, and it took Columbus to bring them to our shores.

Leeks were cultivated in Egypt from around 2000 B.C. and were probably the onions the fleeing Israelites missed so much, as described in the Book of Exodus in the Old Testament. In A.D. 640 Welsh soldiers wore them on their armor to distinguish themselves from enemy Saxons. They won the battle, and today the Welsh wear a leek on St. David's Day to commemorate the victory.

Garlic, perhaps the most pungent member of the onion family, has been suggested as a cold fighter, painkiller, insect repellent, even, when worn around the neck, as protection against vampires. But for me, all these possible uses pale by comparison to the most obvious — that of a flavor enhancer.

■ FRANCA'S ROAST GARLIC PASTA

1 firm, large head of garlic

5 tablespoons extra-virgin olive oil

4 very ripe, juicy tomatoes, peeled

1 small carrot, peeled and minced fine

1 small onion, chopped fine

1/4 cup red wine

Generous pinch of granulated sugar

2 anchovy fillets, mashed to a paste, or 1 teaspoon anchovy paste

2 tablespoons imported tomato paste

1 tablespoon heavy or sour cream

1/4 cup freshly grated Parmesan cheese, plus more for passing

1 cup loosely packed fresh basil, leaves only

1/4 cup pitted Ligurian or niçoise olives

Salt and freshly ground black pepper

1 pound penne or other pasta

When I lived in Rome, I had an inspired cook who soon became my friend and mentor. Franca came from a small village in the mountains of southern Italy, so she used meat sparingly. With a look of disapproval, she would accuse me of extravagance when I returned from the market with twelve ounces of meat. She did not, however, stint on vegetables and prepared them in ways I had never imagined. This pasta dish is a close approximation of one of Franca's recipes. Redolent of garlic, it brought lip-smacking compliments from even blasé Romans.

Preheat the oven to 425°F.

Slice the top of the garlic head, cutting through each clove. Place the head in a small baking pan, cut side down, drizzle with 2 tablespoons of the olive oil, and bake 30 minutes or until the cloves are very tender when a toothpick is inserted. Set aside.

Put the tomatoes in the bowl of a food processor fitted with a steel blade and pulse to chop small. Do not purée. Set aside.

In a medium-sized nonstick skillet, heat 2 tablespoons of the oil, add the carrot and onion, and sauté, stirring until the vegetables are very soft. Add the tomatoes, wine, and sugar. Cook 5 minutes, over low to moderate heat, stirring occasionally. Add the anchovies and tomato paste and mix completely. Simmer until the sauce begins to thicken.

Separate the garlic cloves, squeeze the garlic into a small bowl, add the heavy cream, and mash into a paste. Stir into the tomato sauce and mix thoroughly.

Remove from the heat and stir in 1/4 cup of the cheese, half of the chopped basil, and the olives. Correct seasoning with salt and pepper.

Cook the pasta until *al dente* in plenty of boiling salted

water. Drain it thoroughly and return to the empty cooking pot. Dry the pasta over low heat.

Add the final tablespoon of olive oil and toss.

Transfer the pasta to a warm serving dish, add the last half of the basil, and toss.

Pour half the sauce on the pasta and toss to coat. Grate some additional Parmesan cheese over the top and serve.

Pass the remaining sauce and additional cheese.

Serves 8, with sauce to spare

■ NOT SO TRADITIONAL LIVER AND ONION

Many of us have stricken red meat from our menus for health reasons. Yet liver is a great source of iron. If eaten as a treat and in moderation, this delicious traditional food can be included in almost any diet. I prefer this low-fat version, which is made even tastier by the addition of fresh sorrel from my garden. Mashed potatoes are the perfect accompaniment.

In a nonstick skillet, heat 1 tablespoon of the oil. Add the onion and cook, stirring occasionally, until the onion is tender. Add the liver, salt, and pepper, and sauté, stirring until the meat is no longer pink and is cooked through.

With a slotted spoon remove the onion and liver to a serving platter and keep warm. Working quickly, add the final tablespoon of oil and heat over a low flame. Add the sorrel and toss until just wilted. Add 2 tablespoons light cream and deglaze the pan. Pour over the liver and toss.

Serves 6

2 tablespoons extra-virgin olive oil

1 large onion, cut in half and sliced thin, lengthwise

1½ pounds calf's liver, cut into ½-inch-wide strips

1 teaspoon kosher salt

¼ teaspoon freshly ground black pepper

1 bunch sorrel (about 13 leaves), stems trimmed and leaves cut in strips

2 tablespoons light cream

■ CURRIED LEEK AND RICE SALAD

2 cups cooked basmati rice

1 cup cooked wild rice

2 leeks

1 can artichoke hearts

½ cup dark raisins

½ cup toasted slivered almonds

Dressing

¾ cup mayonnaise

Juice of 1 lemon

1 tablespoon chives, snipped with
    a scissors, not chopped

1 tablespoon parsley, snipped
    with a scissors, not chopped

2 teaspoons salt

1 teaspoon white pepper

1 teaspoon curry paste

Before cooking leeks it's important to wash them thoroughly. Cut them vertically about an inch from the base but not through it. Swirl the cut leeks in a bowl of cold water or under running water. Drain them thoroughly.

Leeks give this salad a subtle flavor that works well with the complicated taste of the curry. It's an excellent side dish with simple grilled fish or meat and you can prepare it a day in advance.

Place cooled, cooked rice into a large bowl.

Trim the green leaves of the leeks down to about 2 inches from the top of the white part. Discard the green parts and wash the rest as described above. Pull off the two outer leaves and slice the leeks thinly about 4 inches from the bottom. Cut each slice in half. Add the leeks to the rice and toss to mix.

Drain the artichoke hearts and dry them on paper towels. Remove about half the leaves from each one and discard them. Cut the resulting artichoke hearts and bottoms into 6 parts. Combine the raisins, almonds, and artichokes, and add to the rice. Toss gently to mix.

Combine all the dressing ingredients and whisk until completely mixed.

Add the dressing to the rice salad a little at a time, mix, taste, and add more dressing as needed.

Chill.

Serves 6 to 8

■ GRANDMA MORSE'S FINISHING SAUCE

Ken Morse is a shipbuilder in Maine. In 1996 he submitted his grandmother's barbecue sauce to the "Best Ribs" competition at the "Pig and Pepper" festival in Carlisle, Massachusetts, and won first prize. The Pig and Pepper draws rib enthusiasts from all over the world to compete or just to "pig out" to their hearts' content.

In the parlance of the barbecue world, Mr. Morse tells us, his grandmother's concoction is called a "finishing sauce." I call it a heroic way to use homegrown garlic.

1 cup spring water

2 cups ketchup

1 cup dark brown sugar

1½ cups apple cider vinegar

3 medium onions, chopped

25 cloves garlic, peeled and lightly crushed

8 teaspoons Worcestershire sauce

4 tablespoons salt

2 tablespoons freshly ground black pepper

Combine all the ingredients in a saucepan and bring to a boil. Lower the heat and simmer the sauce for about 3 hours, stirring occasionally. The onions will be translucent.

Refrigerate until needed.

Yields approximately 4 cups

Hints for barbecuing from the champion

1. Ask your butcher for "3½ pounds and down" racks of ribs for whatever number of guests you are having. The butcher will tell you how many racks you will need.

2. Be sure to remove the membrane from the bone side of the rack. The butcher can do this for you, or you can do it with a fork and a piece of paper towel to grab it. If you don't, the ribs may be bitter.

3. In the barbecuing world, *barbecue* means "smoking," but an oven may be used. You will need a rib rack for either smoker or oven method, placing the ribs fat side up.

4. If you use a smoker, use applewood only. Smoke at 200°F for 4½ hours. Fill a spray bottle with 50 percent apple cider vinegar and 50 percent apple juice and spray the ribs every 20 minutes. When done, separate the ribs with a cleaver and put them on a platter. Pour the sauce over the ribs.

5. If you plan to use the oven, bake for 15 minutes in a 400°F preheated oven. Turn the oven down to 250°F and bake for 5 hours. In the last hour, brush the ribs with the sauce every 15 minutes. Serve as you would the smoked ribs. Serve extra sauce with both methods.

CHAPTER 12
PEAS

Peas begin to lose their sweetness soon after harvest, so it is not surprising that peas purchased in the supermarket have only the mildest flavor. Gardeners have an advantage over nongardeners in that they can pick peas just before using them and can cultivate the three varieties that make cooking so exciting these days.

Traditional plants have fully mature, tender, sweet peas inside a tough and usually inedible pod. Peas with edible pods, like snow peas, are harvested when the pea inside is very small and undeveloped. And the snap pea gives you the best of the other two; it has a tender and delicious pod and sweet, delicate full-sized peas inside.

■ FRESH PEA PILAF WITH GREEN WHEAT AND PISTACHIOS

*Here is another recipe from the kitchen of Ana Sortun of
Casablanca in Cambridge, Massachusetts. She tells us that the
secret to this pilaf is sweet fresh peas. And because peas, like corn,
begin to lose their sweetness soon after harvesting, the gardening
cook will be able to taste the true flavor of this wonderful dish.
If you pick peas every day during the harvest season, you will
encourage more growth.*

 *This pilaf is easy to prepare but requires time to shuck the
peas and wash the green wheat.*

Heat plenty of oil and butter in a very large skillet. When
hot and bubbly, add vermicelli pieces and stir constantly until
golden brown. Adjust the heat if they are browning too quickly.
Drain off excess grease and set aside.

Run green wheat under cold water in a bowl and skim off
any excess wheat kernels that come to the top. Soak for at least
10 minutes. Drain and sort through grain by grain, checking
for little black pebbles. Set the wheat aside.

Rinse the bulghur and set aside.

In a large saucepan melt about 1 tablespoon of butter with
3 tablespoons of olive oil. Sauté the onion and pistachios until
the onion is translucent. Add noodles and 1 cup water. Cook
until the noodles absorb the water and aren't crunchy. Stir in
the green wheat and bulghur and season with salt and freshly
ground pepper, add another cup of water, and continue to cook
until the wheat is tender but not puffed. You may need a little
more water.

Remove from heat and stir the peas into the hot pilaf.
Correct seasoning and add parsley.

Yields about 8 cups

Extra-virgin olive oil and
 unsalted butter

1 cup vermicelli, broken into
 little pieces

1 cup green wheat, also called
 firik (available in Middle
 Eastern markets)

1 cup dark, coarse (not fine)
 bulghur

1 yellow onion, minced

1 cup pistachio pieces

Salt and freshly ground black
 pepper

1 cup freshly shucked English
 peas

1/2 bunch fresh parsley, finely
 chopped

■ TARRAGON PEAS AND CARROTS

2 tablespoons unsalted butter

3 cups baby carrots

1 tablespoon light brown sugar

1/8 teaspoon ground cinnamon

1/2 cup freshly shucked peas

Generous pinch of kosher salt

1 sprig fresh tarragon

I can still remember how I resisted eating those tasteless soggy carrots and overcooked peas that the school lunch monitor pressed on us. Neither the carrots nor the peas had any relation to the wonderful fresh vegetables from our home garden.

There is no more delicious vegetable than peas freshly picked and shucked. However, because they begin to lose their sugar almost immediately after they're harvested, it is best to wait until you are ready to use them.

In a nonstick saucepan or skillet for which you have a tight cover, heat the butter until it bubbles. Add the carrots and toss to coat. Add the sugar and cinnamon and stir 1 minute. Cover and cook, shaking the pan, for 2 minutes longer. Add the peas and stir. Cover and cook over high heat, shaking the pan frequently for 25 minutes longer. Both peas and carrots will be crunchy. If you like them more tender cook them for an additional 15 minutes.

Toss the vegetables with the kosher salt and transfer them to a serving platter and, with kitchen scissors, snip the tarragon over the vegetables.

Serve immediately.

Serves 6

■ SESAME SUGAR SNAP PEAS

Sugar snap peas often taste so good right from the vine that the harvest sometimes doesn't make it to the pot. I think you'll find that this adaptation of a recipe by Paul Sussman, the chef at Daddy-O's Cafe in Cambridge, Massachusetts, retains all the just-picked flavor and more.

1 pound sugar snap peas

1 teaspoon sesame oil

1 tablespoon light soy sauce

1 tablespoon freshly squeezed orange juice

1 teaspoon granulated sugar

¼ teaspoon distilled vinegar

Radicchio leaves for garnish (optional)

1 tablespoon toasted sesame seeds

Remove the strings from the peas. Wash and pat dry.

Put peas in a small bowl, add the sesame oil, and toss to coat thoroughly. Cover and set aside.

In a small bowl, combine the soy sauce, orange juice, sugar, and vinegar. Whisk until the sugar is completely dissolved. Set aside.

Heat a heavy-bottomed or seasoned cast-iron skillet over high heat. Add the peas and toss until some are slightly brown and the others are highly colored. Turn out and set aside.

Quickly wilt the radicchio, if desired, in the same skillet and turn it out onto a large serving dish or individual plates. Spoon the peas over the radicchio. They are meant to be eaten at slightly above room temperature.

Sprinkle a little of the soy-orange sauce on the peas and sprinkle with the sesame seeds. Pass the remaining sauce at the table.

Serves 6 to 8

CHAPTER 13
PEPPERS

Salsa, made from both hot and sweet peppers, has overtaken ketchup as the favorite American condiment.

Capsicum is the species of pepper to which both sweet peppers and hot peppers belong. The people of Central and South America, the Caribbean, and Mexico used peppers in their cuisine as early as 7000 B.C.; in 1492 Columbus took capsicum plants back to Europe, and before long peppers were being grown in Africa and Asia. They soon became more important in Asia than black pepper, which until then had been the dominant spice.

Handling chili peppers requires special care. Always use rubber gloves and never touch your eyes or nose with the gloves once you've handled the peppers.

The seeds are the hottest part of the pepper, and many recipes ask you to remove them. Cut off the stem. Slice the pepper lengthwise, carefully remove the seeds and membranes, and discard them.

Roasted peppers, often called for in recipes, are easy to prepare. If the pepper is a chili pepper, then don't forget to use rubber gloves. To roast chili or sweet peppers, place them directly on the flame of the stove or two inches from the broiler. When the skin has burned, turn the pepper and repeat the process until the entire pepper is charred. Place the pepper in a paper bag and close it. Let it stand for 10 minutes. Remove it and peel the black skin. It will pull away easily. Remove the stem, seeds, and membranes, and cut the pepper into quarters. It is now ready to use.

■ TROPICAL FRUIT AND PEPPER SALSA

Technically, tomatoes are fruits that originated in tropical America, so combining them with mangoes and papayas seems a perfectly natural thing to do. But no salsa is worth its name without the balancing taste of peppers, and so I've added both sweet and hot peppers to make this surprisingly different relish.

  Serve it with grilled fish or meat, and you'll get rave notices.

In a stainless-steel bowl, combine all the ingredients and mix. Taste and correct seasoning. Chill at least 2 hours before using.

  This salsa will keep in the refrigerator for 1 week, or in the freezer for several months.

  Yields about 1½ cups

2 medium very ripe tomatoes, peeled and coarsely chopped

2 large mangoes, peeled, seeded, and puréed

1 small ripe Hawaiian papaya, peeled, seeded, and cut into small cubes

1 small red bell pepper, stemmed, membranes and seeds removed, and chopped small

½ cup red onion, chopped

2 canned chipotle chili peppers in adobo sauce, minced (available in Latin markets and many supermarkets)

2 teaspoons granulated sugar dissolved in the

Juice of 3 large ripe limes, approximately ½ cup

¼ chopped fresh cilantro

½ teaspoon ground cumin

Salt

■ CHILES RELLENOS

6 long light green Italian sweet
   peppers, lightly roasted and set
   aside to cool in a paper bag

Refried Beans

2 cans red kidney beans, rinsed
   and drained, or 3/4 pound
   dried kidney beans, soaked
   overnight and cooked in water
   to cover until soft, 1 or more
   hours

2 thick slices bacon, cut into small
   pieces

1/2 teaspoon granulated sugar

3 or more tablespoons whole milk

Filling

2 Mexican chorizos, Portuguese
   chouriços, or spicy Italian
   sausages

3 tablespoons extra-virgin olive oil

1 tablespoon unsalted butter

1 onion, chopped fine

3 cloves garlic, chopped fine

1 1/2 cups fresh corn kernels, from
   about 6 small ears

1/2 roasted red bell pepper,
   chopped very fine

2 cups shredded Monterey Jack
   cheese

Fresh cilantro, for garnish

In the last decade Americans have fallen in love with peppers. We grow them, we eat them, we plant them, we decorate almost anything that doesn't move with pictures of them, and, of course, we stuff them. Stuffed peppers are found in one form or other in most of the world's cuisines.

In Mexico, long sweet peppers are usually filled with white cheese, then dipped in an egg-and-flour batter and fried. This variation on the Mexican chile relleno (stuffed chili pepper) does not require deep frying and benefits from the sun-ripened flavors of the vegetables.

With a tossed salad and hot corn tortillas, this recipe makes a great lunch.

Slit open the roasted Italian peppers lengthwise, 1/4 inch from the top to about a 1/2 inch from the bottom. Pull out the seeds but leave the stems and the peppers intact. Set aside.

To prepare the refried beans, mash the drained beans until almost smooth and set aside.

In a nonstick skillet, cook the bacon until crisp. Add the beans and fry, stirring continually until they begin to bubble. Stir in the sugar and the milk, one tablespoon at a time, until a smooth, not too thin, paste is produced. Set aside and keep warm.

To prepare the filling, remove the meat from the sausage casing and crumble. Set aside.

In a medium skillet, heat the oil and butter until bubbly. Add the onion and garlic and cook, stirring, until tender. Add the corn and stir 1 minute. Add the red pepper and sausage. Cook, stirring, until the meat is cooked through, about 10 minutes.

Half fill the peppers with this mixture. Then fill the remaining space with cheese. Place the peppers on a broiler pan about 5 inches from the heat. Broil just until the cheese melts. Keep warm.

To serve, spread refried beans on each of 6 plates. Place one pepper in the center of each plate. Mound additional cheese on the peppers and snip cilantro with a scissors over all. Serve immediately.

Serves 6

■ PINEAPPLE-PEPPER GUACAMOLE

2 ripe plum tomatoes, peeled,
    seeded, and quartered

1 small onion, peeled and
    quartered

1 clove garlic, minced fine

1 canned chipotle pepper in
    adobo sauce, chopped
    (available in Latin markets
    and many supermarkets)

½ cup fresh cilantro leaves

⅓ fresh pineapple, peeled,
    cored, and cut into ½-inch
    slices

1 large or 2 small ripe avocados,
    peeled, pitted, and mashed

½ roasted red bell pepper,
    peeled and chopped fine

Juice of 1 lime

Salt

Tradition takes a sharp turn with the addition of pineapple in this recipe. Roasted peppers and plum tomatoes combine with many contrasting tastes and textures to make this guacamole an interesting appetizer or accompaniment. Try it on fresh tomato slices, with fish, or with any surplus from your garden, steamed or sautéed.

In the bowl of a food processor fitted with a steel blade, combine the tomatoes, onion, garlic, chipotle pepper, and cilantro leaves, and pulse 4 or 5 times until you have small chunks.

Cut the pineapple slices from the center to the outer edge, into thin matchstick slices. Set aside.

In a stainless-steel bowl, combine the processed vegetables, the avocados, bell peppers, and pineapple. Add half the lime juice, mix in, and taste. Add more lime juice to taste. Correct seasoning with salt.

Yields 1 to 1½ cups

CHAPTER 14
POTATOES

Although for a long time potatoes were scorned as fodder or food for the poor, home gardeners and small farmers have developed a great interest in planting new varieties of potatoes and in the recultivation of old ones.

The history of the potato is long and complicated. Archaeologists found the remains of wild varieties in Chile dating from 11,000 B.C. and cultivated ones from around 5000 B.C. In the sixteenth century, Spanish conquistadors brought the plant to Europe, where it traveled throughout the continent, as well as Ireland and England, where it was used as animal fodder.

We can thank the arrival of Irish immigrants in the nineteenth century, and the Mormons moving west to Utah and Idaho, for the cultivation and spread of potatoes as food for human consumption.

Baking and boiling potatoes can be found today in every supermarket, but the more interesting varieties, such as red bliss, German fingerlings, and Yukon golds, are available in few supermarkets or in specialty produce stores.

■ POTATO KUGEL WITH ARTICHOKES

1 cup canned artichoke hearts

1 cup egg whites and yolks, from about 4 jumbo eggs

1 teaspoon salt

1/2 teaspoon freshly ground black pepper

1/4 cup canola or light extra-virgin olive oil, plus more for oiling the pan

2 medium onions

4 large (about 3 pounds) waxy potatoes, peeled and kept in water to cover

1 small tomato, sliced very thin

1/3 cup freshly grated Parmesan cheese

As children growing up in Mexico, my brother and I knew exactly where we would be every Sunday. Lunch with grandparents was a command performance rather than a meal. The entire clan, numbering eleven, gathered to eat a traditional Jewish family meal. The menu changed often, but we could always count on a potato kugel. This variation on Abuelita Libnic's perennial delight is hearty enough to serve as a main course with salad.

Preheat the oven to 350°F.

Drain the artichoke hearts and cut them into strips. Reserve.

In a large mixing bowl, combine the eggs, salt, pepper, and oil, and mix.

Fit a food processor with a coarse grating disk and grate the onions.

Add the grated onions to the eggs and mix.

With the same disk, grate the potatoes and immediately add them to the egg-onion mixture. Combine and set aside.

Oil a 12½-by-8½-inch baking dish. Turn half of the potato mixture into the pan and pat lightly to level it. Add two-thirds of the artichoke slices and spread them over the potatoes. Add the remaining potato mixture and pat to level. Sprinkle the remaining artichokes over the top and arrange the tomato slices over them.

Bake 1 hour. Sprinkle the cheese over the top and raise the heat to 450°F. Bake an additional 5 to 10 minutes or until golden brown. Do not let the cheese burn.

Remove the pan from the oven and allow to cool a bit before serving.

Serves 6 to 8

■ POTATO PUDDINGS WITH ROASTED PEPPERS

Though the potato is the mainstay of this dish, onion, red pepper, and spinach add both color and sensational tastes. And the individual puddings are flavorful accompaniments to almost any entrée.

Preheat the oven to 350°F.

Over medium heat, in a small nonstick skillet, heat slightly 1 tablespoon of the oil. Add the onion and sauté, stirring, until transparent. Remove from skillet, set aside, and cool.

Place the spinach in a saucepan for which you have a tight-fitting top. If the spinach is quite dry before cooking, add 1 teaspoon water to the saucepan and cook over medium heat until the spinach is just wilted. Chop, drain, and set aside.

Slice the pepper into julienne strips, setting aside 8 strips for garnish.

Grate the potatoes coarsely, drain, and set aside.

Combine the eggs, salt, pepper, sautéed onions, and the remaining oil in a large bowl and whisk until the salt is dissolved. Add the potatoes and mix to combine completely.

Oil well 8 individual timbales or soufflé cups. Fill each halfway with the potato mixture. Using half the feta, crumble some cheese into each cup. Place the chopped spinach on the cheese, top with all but eight strips of the red pepper, and sprinkle on the remaining cheese. Add the remaining potato mixture and spread.

Place the cups on a cookie sheet and bake in the preheated oven for 50 minutes or until slightly brown. Raise the heat to 450°F for 5 to 10 minutes or until golden brown.

Remove from the heat and garnish each pudding with a strip of red pepper and a cilantro leaf.

Serves 8

3 tablespoons extra-virgin green (Greek or Spanish) olive oil

1 medium Spanish onion, grated and drained

2 ounces young spinach, washed and spun dry

1 roasted red bell pepper, peeled and seeded

3 medium baking potatoes, peeled and kept in water to cover

3 large eggs, lightly beaten

1 teaspoon salt

1/2 teaspoon freshly ground black pepper

1/3 cup crumbled feta cheese

8 fresh cilantro leaves for garnish (optional)

CHAPTER 15
PUMPKIN

Few plants are easier to grow than pumpkins, but most gardeners are afraid they are not suitable for small plots. That is no longer true. Varieties of this delicious winter squash range from one pound to the two-hundred-pound competition types. Pick a variety that fits your garden and your needs.

Whether you choose to grow your own pumpkins or buy them in the market, you will find that the following recipes will make for splendid eating.

■ SWEET PUMPKIN GNOCCHI

*Americans have taken potato gnocchi with cheese and tomato sauce
to their culinary hearts. But in Italy, there are as many varieties
of gnocchi as there are regions. Venetians eat gnocchi made with
pumpkin or other winter squash, and serve them for dessert.
Surprise your family and friends, who'll be sure to ask for seconds.*

Place the pumpkin into a pot for which you have a lid,
add water to cover, and bring to a boil. Reduce the heat to medium-
low, cover, and simmer until very soft.

Drain the pumpkin until quite dry and put through a ricer or
into a food processor fitted with a plastic blade or mash with a fork.
Process until the squash resembles mashed potatoes without lumps.
Set aside until just warm to the touch.

Preheat the oven to 350°F.

Beat the egg yolks and whisk into the cooled squash. Add
1/2 teaspoon kosher salt and mix in. With clean, dry beaters, whisk
the egg whites until soft peaks are formed and gently fold them into
the squash.

Little by little, fold in the flour-cornmeal mixture. Add only
enough flour to make a firm but not hard dough. Form the dough
into foot-long rolls about 1 or 2 inches thick and pinch off or cut
into pieces about 1/2 inch thick.

Put the dumplings in a very large pot filled with boiling salted
water and boil until they rise to the surface. Skim them onto a baking
sheet covered with layers of paper towel to drain. Do not overcook them.

When all the gnocchi are boiled and drained, turn them into a
buttered baking dish that will accommodate them all in one layer, dot
with more butter, and place the dish into a larger one. Fill the outer
dish with boiling water to come about two-thirds of the way up the
sides of the dumpling dish (a bain-marie). Bake for 10 minutes.
Sprinkle with the cinnamon-sugar-clove mixture.

Serve immediately, mounded on a dessert plate, with vanilla ice
cream or whipped cream on the side.

Serves 6 to 8

2 cups pumpkin or other winter squash, such as acorn or buttercup, peeled and cubed

2 jumbo eggs, separated

Kosher salt

1/2 cup all-purpose flour, sifted together with

1/2 cup fine cornmeal or 1 cup semolina flour

4 tablespoons butter cut into 1/4-inch cubes, plus more for greasing the pan

2 tablespoons granulated sugar mixed with

1 teaspoon ground cinnamon and a pinch of ground cloves

■ PUMPKIN CHOCOLATE CHIP CAKE

Streusel Topping

¼ cup granulated sugar

¼ cup light brown sugar

¼ cup all-purpose flour

¼ cup chopped walnuts

2 tablespoons unsalted butter

1 teaspoon ground cinnamon

Cake

1 stick (8 ounces) unsalted butter,
  at room temperature

½ cup granulated sugar

½ cup light brown sugar

2 large eggs

1 cup cooked pumpkin

1 teaspoon vanilla

2 cups all-purpose flour

2 teaspoons baking powder

1½ teaspoons ground cinnamon

½ teaspoon baking soda

½ teaspoon salt

¼ teaspoon ground ginger

¼ teaspoon ground nutmeg

¼ cup miniature chocolate chips

If you don't have pumpkins, you can make this cake with any other fresh, canned, or frozen winter squash.

To make the streusel topping, in a bowl combine all the topping ingredients and mix well. Set aside.

To make the cake, preheat the oven to 350°F.

In a food processor or electric mixer, cream the butter with the sugars. Add the eggs, pumpkin, and vanilla. Add the remaining ingredients, except the chocolate chips, and beat to combine.

Pour the batter into a greased 10-inch springform pan, sprinkle with chocolate chips, cover with streusel.

Bake for 45 minutes.

Cool the cake on a rack before removing it from the pan.

Serves 8 to 10

■ PUMPKIN IN SYRUP

I first tasted this delicious dessert at a restaurant overlooking the Bosporous in Istanbul. When I asked the chef what it was, he proudly replied, "Turkish pumpkin." Since that time I've learned that many cultures, Afghan and Lebanese, among others, claim this dish as their own.

To make the syrup, combine the sugar, honey, 1/4 cup water, lemon juice, and rind in a stainless-steel or enameled saucepan. Bring to a boil over medium-high heat and stir occasionally. Do not allow to burn. Boil about 3 minutes.

Stir in the rose and orange blossom waters and boil to a slow count of 15. Set aside. If the syrup thickens or hardens before you are ready to use it, add 1 tablespoon water and stir it over low heat until it becomes thinner.

Preheat the oven to 375°F.

Place the squash pieces in a saucepan that will hold them in one layer. Add water just to cover. Add the butter and salt and bring to a boil. Lower the heat and simmer until the squash is tender.

Drain the squash thoroughly and transfer it to a buttered baking dish. Brush only the edible portions with some syrup and bake for 20 minutes. Remove the dish from the oven, pour the remaining syrup over the squash, and set aside to cool to room temperature.

Divide the squash among 6 plates, spoon some syrup over it, and sprinkle with the walnuts. Serve.

Serves 6

Syrup

3/4 cup granulated sugar

1 tablespoon honey

1/2 teaspoon freshly squeezed lemon juice

1 teaspoon grated lemon rind

1/2 tablespoon rosewater (available in Middle Eastern markets and many supermarkets)

1/2 tablespoon orange blossom water (available in Middle Eastern markets and many supermarkets)

Pumpkin

3 miniature pumpkins, stems and seeds removed, quartered, or 12 slices buttercup squash or acorn squash

2 tablespoons unsalted butter

1/4 teaspoon salt

1/2 cup toasted walnuts, coarsely chopped

CHAPTER 16
SUMMER SQUASH
Crookneck
and Zucchini

Crookneck squash, a nutty-flavored summer squash, is often overshadowed by its more popular cousin the zucchini. Yet crookneck squash is as easy to grow and as prolific as zucchini and can often be used interchangeably in cooking. In addition to its pleasant flavor, the crookneck can be counted on to add a warm, sunny color to the presentation of any dish.

Zucchini, like crookneck squash, belongs to the genus *Cururbita,* of which some of the oldest remains have been found in Mexico, where it formed an integral part of the pre-Columbian diet. The zucchini itself was probably introduced to America with the Italian immigration of the nineteenth century and is now as much a part of the American diet as broccoli or lettuce.

Most gardeners plant too many zucchini, and at end of summer a heavy traffic in free zucchini, often of prodigious size, develops. Better resist the urge to cultivate more than two or three zucchini plants or be prepared to join the parade of neighbors trying to give away their surplus.

■ STUFFED CROOKNECK SQUASH

Sauce

3 ripe tomatoes, peeled, seeded, and chopped

2 scallions, trimmed, white and 2 inches of green, sliced

½ cup kalamata olives, pitted and minced

½ cup black olives, minced

½ cup red wine

1 tablespoon tomato paste

Squash

3 medium crookneck squash

1 teaspoon sea salt or kosher salt

Olive oil

Stuffing

¾ pound sweet Italian sausage

2 slices, ½ inch thick, sweet onion, such as Vidalia or Walla Walla, chopped

5 ounces of young spinach, stems removed and torn into salad-sized pieces

15 ounces ricotta cheese

Salt and freshly ground black pepper

½ cup shelled, chopped pistachio nuts (optional)

Weekend gardeners find summer squash particularly satisfying because most varieties now grow on bush plants instead of vines and tend to produce a profusion of fruit. One plant per family member should be sufficient to keep everyone happy.

Though this recipe was developed for crookneck squash, you can substitute some of your larger zucchini or any summer squash large enough to stuff. And you can make the sauce, which gives the squash both color and piquancy, in advance and refrigerate it.

To make the sauce, put tomatoes, scallions, olives, and ¼ cup of the wine in a small saucepan. Bring just to a boil and lower the heat. Simmer about 3 minutes or until most of the wine is absorbed. Add the tomato paste, the remaining wine, and ¾ cup water.

Simmer, stirring occasionally, until thickened.

Set the sauce aside or refrigerate it if you don't plan to use it immediately.

To prepare the squash, heat a large pot of water with the salt.

Roll the squash around to find the natural "seat." Cut it in half lengthwise, and, using a melon scoop or grapefruit spoon, scoop out the seeds and discard. Be careful not to cut through the bottom.

Blanch the shells in boiling water for 1 minute, then immerse them in cold water to stop the cooking. Drain and place the shells on a cookie sheet brushed with olive oil.

Preheat the oven to 400°F.

To make the stuffing, remove the casing from the sausage. Brown the meat in a dry nonstick skillet, until it's thoroughly cooked and easy to crumble.

Add the onions and cook until soft. Add the spinach and cook until just wilted.

Turn off the heat, add the cheese, mix, and correct the

seasoning with salt and pepper to taste. Stir in the nuts if you
desire them.

Fill the shells with the sausage mixture and bake 20
minutes.

To finish the dish, reheat the sauce. Place each cooked
squash shell on a dinner plate and spoon the sauce over the
middle, forming a cross with the squash. The white stuffing
should show on either end.

Serves 6

■ COURGETTES DE GENEVIEVE

*Zucchini growers all have at least one recipe in their files like this
one. No one remembers where it came from or when he first tried it,
but it doesn't really matter. It has become a family favorite. And it
wouldn't surprise me if this one becomes one of yours.*

4 large zucchini, about 2 pounds, grated and drained

1½ cups boiled brown rice

½ cup coarsely chopped walnuts

3 tablespoons unsalted butter, cut into small ½-inch cubes, plus more for the casserole

4 large eggs, lightly beaten

½ cup whole milk

1½ teaspoons kosher salt

¼ teaspoon freshly ground black pepper

1 teaspoon sweet paprika

Preheat the oven to 350°F.

Gently squeeze as much liquid as possible out of the grated
zucchini. In a large bowl, combine the zucchini, rice, and
walnuts and mix thoroughly.

Butter a 9-by-13-inch baking dish. Put the zucchini mix into
the baking dish and spread evenly.

In a small bowl combine the eggs, milk, salt, pepper, and
paprika. Mix until the salt is dissolved and the paprika is
completely incorporated.

Pour the eggs and milk over the zucchini mixture and dot all
over with the 3 tablespoons butter.

Bake for 20 minutes or until the casserole becomes brown
and crisp around the edges.

Serves 6 to 8

■ FIOR DI ZUCCHINE FRITTI

Pastella (Batter)

2 large eggs

1½ tablespoons olive oil

½ teaspoon salt

¾ cup all-purpose flour

Zucchini Flowers

18 zucchini flowers

1 pound whole-milk
    mozzarella

18 anchovy fillets

Vegetable oil for frying

When I asked Franco Romagnoli, the talented Italian cookbook author, television personality, and one-time restaurateur, to name his favorite vegetable dish, he immediately replied, "fior di zucchine."

Zucchini flowers are ready for plucking about fifteen days before the zucchini is ready for harvesting. They are a delicacy that gardeners enjoy almost exclusively because the flower is generally too delicate to be picked, packaged, and sent to markets.

Here is Franco's recipe.

To make the batter, break the eggs into a bowl, add the oil, ⅔ cup warm water, and salt. Beat until nicely mixed and homogeneous. Slowly sprinkle in the flour, beating constantly, until the mixture has the consistency of a good pancake batter. Let it sit for a couple of hours before using.

To prepare the flowers, remove the pistils inside the flowers and cut off any discolored or wilted parts of the petals. Wash carefully in very cold water and set out to dry on paper towels. Dice the mozzarella, and cut each anchovy into 3 or 4 pieces. Open the petals of the flowers, put in 3 or 4 cubes of cheese, 3 or 4 bits of anchovy, or just enough to fill but not to overstuff.

Heat the frying oil to 375°F (or hot enough so that a drop of batter frizzles on contact). Gently dip the flowers into the batter, one by one, coating them well, and immediately fry them, a few at a time, to a golden brown. Drain on paper towels and serve hot as an appetizer.

Serves 6

■ CHRIS'S GREEN BREAD

It would appear that every gardener has a recipe for zucchini bread. The artist Christina Le Fevre, my very talented assistant, developed this tasty masterpiece some time ago. In Chris's home, this easy and delicious way of using the annual bounty of zucchini is known as green bread, and it is consumed almost as soon as it comes out of the oven. It's also a great way to use up a zucchini harvest because you can freeze the breads.

Preheat the oven to 350°F.

Slice the zucchini in half lengthwise and remove the seeds. Do not peel.

Cut each length into 1/2-inch slices and boil them in slightly salted water until soft. Drain and set aside.

Sift together the flour, baking powder, baking soda, and 1/2 teaspoon salt.

In the bowl of an electric mixer, cream the shortening and sugar, adding the sugar gradually. Add the eggs and beat to incorporate completely.

While continuing to mix on low, add the dry ingredients alternately with the zucchini. Mix in the walnuts, if desired.

Turn the batter into a greased 8½-by-4½-by-3-inch loaf pan and bake for 1 hour, or until a toothpick inserted in the center comes out clean.

Cool in the pan and serve.

Yields 8 to 10 slices

2 medium zucchini

1/2 teaspoon salt, plus more for the zucchini water

1¾ cups all-purpose flour

2 teaspoons baking powder

1/4 teaspoon baking soda

1/3 cup solid vegetable shortening

2/3 cup granulated sugar

2 large eggs, lightly beaten

1/2 cup chopped walnuts (optional)

▪ GARDEN GRIDDLE CAKES

1 cup whole milk

½ cup skim milk, plus more to thin the batter

1 teaspoon granulated sugar

1 tablespoon sour cream, plus more to dollop on the griddle cakes

1 cup coarsely grated zucchini, sprinkled with

½ teaspoon salt, and drained

½ cup grated carrots

½ cup fresh corn kernels

1 small onion, minced fine

1 small clove garlic, minced fine

Several grinds black pepper

2 tablespoons extra-virgin olive oil, plus more to grease the skillet

1 cup stone-ground precooked white cornmeal (available in Latin markets and many supermarkets)

2 tablespoons melted unsalted butter, cooled

2 jumbo eggs, lightly beaten

Salsa

During World War II, American schoolchildren were encouraged to plant vegetables in boxes or backyards. A successful garden, we were assured, would help bring victory. My patriotic efforts produced a few rather puny radishes, but my zucchini were remarkable. No one will ever convince me that the Allied victory was not achieved, at least in part, by my first success as a gardener.

Combine the whole milk, skim milk, sugar, and 1 tablespoon sour cream in a glass bowl and heat in the microwave on medium-low for 1 minute or leave in a warm (below 150°F) oven for 10 minutes or until the milk mixture is room temperature to the touch. Set aside.

Combine the salted zucchini, carrots, corn, onion, garlic, and pepper. Mix gently.

Add the 2 tablespoons oil to a medium-sized skillet, heat, and add the vegetables. Sauté them, stirring, until the onions are soft. Do not allow the vegetables to brown. Remove them from the heat and let stand.

Mix together the cornmeal, milk mixture, melted butter, vegetables, any oil left in the skillet, and the eggs. Allow to stand for 5 minutes. The batter should be thin enough to spread. If it is necessary to thin the batter, add more skim milk, 1 tablespoon at a time, to a maximum of 3 tablespoons.

Grease a cast-iron skillet or griddle lightly with additional oil or spray with nonstick vegetable spray. Heat the skillet or griddle over medium heat, and pour batter on the griddle, about 2 tablespoons per griddle cake, and cook until they start to bubble. Turn and brown the other side.

Serve with additional sour cream and the salsa, guacamole, or relishes in this book.

Yields about 24 cakes

■ GRILLED ZUCCHINI AND TOMATOES

Almost any trattoria in Italy will entice you with a large platter of this dish prominently displayed on a table just outside the door or in the window.

You'll understand why when you try it yourself. It's a wonderfully easy way to treat those surplus zucchini and tomatoes.

5 tablespoons extra-virgin olive oil

2 tablespoons fresh lemon thyme leaves

1 tablespoon sea salt

2 large ripe tomatoes, sliced very thin

5 small zucchini, trimmed and sliced very thin lengthwise

Freshly ground black pepper

2 tablespoons freshly grated Parmesan cheese

Preheat the broiler until red hot.

Brush a large metal gratin dish or cast-iron skillet, or a 12¼-by-8¼-inch aluminum foil baking pan with 1 tablespoon of the oil. Sprinkle 1 tablespoon thyme and ½ tablespoon salt over the oil.

Cover the bottom of the pan with the tomato slices, placing them as close together as possible. Arrange the zucchini slices in overlapping rows down the length of the pan and leave a slight space between rows to allow the tomatoes to show through.

Brush the vegetables with 3 tablespoons of the oil and sprinkle with the remaining thyme and salt.

Drizzle the remaining 1 tablespoon oil over the vegetables and grind fresh black pepper to taste over all.

Place in the broiler 5 inches from the heat and grill until golden brown, about 5 minutes. Remove from the heat and sprinkle with the cheese.

Serve immediately or at room temperature.

Serves 6 to 8

■ SWEET ZUCCHINI RELISH

5 large zucchini, coarsely
    chopped, about 8 cups

1 large Spanish onion, coarsely
    chopped

1 large red onion, coarsely
    chopped

2 large red bell peppers, stems
    removed, seeded, and coarsely
    chopped

4 tablespoons sea salt

Pickling Syrup

2 tablespoons cornstarch softened
    in 1 tablespoon water

2¼ cups cider vinegar

2¼ cups granulated sugar

1 tablespoon mustard powder

1 tablespoon turmeric

½ teaspoon ground nutmeg

½ teaspoon freshly ground black
    pepper

Every summer I find myself wondering what I'm going to do with all the zucchini. I know I'm not alone. You will agree, I'm sure, that no cookbook devoted to garden vegetables can be complete without at least one excellent recipe for preserving this ubiquitous squash. Be sure to freeze it for winter enjoyment.

Mix the vegetables well.

Put a quarter of the vegetables in the bowl of a food processor fitted with a steel blade and pulse about 4 or 5 times until the vegetables are chopped small. Turn them into a large bowl and repeat the process with the rest of the vegetables until they are all chopped small.

Dissolve the salt in 2 cups water. Add it to the vegetables with enough water to cover. Stir to mix.

Cover and allow to stand overnight at cool room temperature.

In a large stainless-steel pot that will hold all the vegetables, combine the pickling ingredients and stir until completely mixed and the sugar is dissolved.

Drain the vegetables and add them to the syrup. Bring to a quick boil, stirring. Lower the heat and simmer 30 minutes, stirring occasionally to prevent burning.

Cool and put into 1-cup containers. Allow a ½-inch air space from the top, cover, and freeze.

The relish will keep in the freezer for 4 to 6 months.

Yields 7 cups

■ Zucchini and Mushrooms Sauté

This dish is particularly delicious if made with young zucchini.

Wash and trim the ends of each zucchini. Slice very thin lengthwise and drain on paper towels.

Slice the mushroom caps about $1/4$-inch thick.

Heat the olive oil over medium heat. Add the garlic and shallots and cook, stirring, until soft. Do not allow them to brown. Add the zucchini and mushrooms and toss to coat. Add the salt and seasoning mix. Cook, stirring occasionally, until the mushrooms have released their liquid and it has been reabsorbed.

Remove from the heat, sprinkle with the lemon juice and oregano. Gently toss, taste, and correct seasoning with salt and freshly ground pepper to taste.

Serves 6

4–6 small zucchini (about 1 lb.)

1–2 very large portobello mushroom caps, weighing about 1 pound

$1/4$ cup olive oil

2 cloves garlic, minced fine

2 cloves shallot, minced fine

$1/2$ teaspoon kosher salt

$1/4$ teaspoon Spicy Seasoning Mix (see p. 110)

Juice of $1/2$ lemon

1 teaspoon chopped fresh oregano

Salt and freshly ground black pepper

CHAPTER 17
TOMATOES

History tells us that tomatoes have taken a very circuitous route to get to American home gardens, but they are most definitely there and usually in profusion.

Today's tomatoes likely evolved from a kind of cherry tomato that grew wild in Peru and Equador, but it was probably in Mexico that it was domesticated. The Spanish conquistadors carried the plant back to Spain in the sixteenth century and before long it had made its way to the rest of Europe.

Some short time after the Revolutionary War, the tomato was introduced to the newly formed United States of America. It is hard to believe that this lovely fruit was looked upon with suspicion. Some believed it to be poisonous while others believed it was an aphrodisiac. It was once called "love apple" or "golden apple," and eaten with some degree of fear.

Now, however, the tomato is one of the most universally eaten vegetables in salads. And it is cooked and processed into innumerable products, from juice to sauce to soups to purée, and on and on. However, it is the sun-ripened tomato, freshly picked from the vine, that provides the most flavor and the greatest pleasure.

To peel tomatoes, fill a large pan with water and bring it to a boil. With a slotted spoon, add the tomatoes one at a time. Blanch each tomato to a count of 3. Remove the tomato and submerge it in ice water to stop the cooking. Remove the stem end and pull the peel from the tomatoes. The same process works, by the way, for peaches and apricots.

■ HONEYED GREEN TOMATO CHUTNEY

Green tomatoes are often the harbingers of fall. A sudden frost reminds us that those left on the vine will probably never ripen. Home gardeners usually end the summer with a surplus of green tomatoes. What, then, to do with them? This chutney is a fine way to enjoy them through the winter.

    In a large stainless-steel or enameled pot, combine all the ingredients and mix thoroughly. Let stand 20 minutes.

    Bring to a boil and lower heat. Simmer slowly, stirring occasionally, about 20 minutes.

    Set aside to cool completely.

    Put into pint freezer containers, cover, date, and freeze.

    Yield will depend on the size of the tomatoes.

6 large green tomatoes, coarsely chopped

2 large onions, coarsely chopped

1 red bell pepper, coarsely chopped

1/2 tablespoon salt

1/2 cup clover, mesquite, or any other favorite honey

1/2 cup white vinegar

1/2 tablespoon mustard seeds, bruised

1/2 tablespoon celery seeds

■ OVEN-DRIED TOMATOES

Zesty Lemon Dressing

2 shallots, minced fine

¼ teaspoon kosher salt

⅛ teaspoon granulated sugar

Freshly grated rind of 1 lemon

Juice of 1 lemon

5 tablespoons extra-virgin olive oil

1–2 pounds plum, cherry, or other
    small tomatoes, halved and
    cored

Olive oil, for storing the tomatoes

Sun-dried tomatoes are a staple in gourmets' diets. They can be purchased in specialty stores dried or preserved in olive oil. If you have a lot of ripe tomatoes that cannot be left on the vine, you can dry them in your own home. This oven-drying method will let you preserve your bumper crop of cherry or plum tomatoes to use for many months after the first frost.

In a small stainless-steel or glass bowl, combine the shallots, salt, and sugar until well combined. Add the rind, juice, and 2 teaspoons water, and whisk until the salt and sugar are completely dissolved, about 60 beats (1 minute).

Whisking continuously, add the olive oil in a slow and steady stream. Whisk an additional 1 minute.

To oven-dry the tomatoes, preheat the oven to 250°F. Whisk the dressing and dip the tomatoes in it.

Place, cut side up, on a grill screen or wire rack on a baking sheet. Bake in the oven for 2 to 3 hours, or until the tomatoes look wrinkled but not dry.

Turn off the oven. Let the tomatoes stand in the oven for an additional 8 hours or until they are firm but not brittle.

You can immerse the tomatoes in olive oil in a tightly closed jar for several months.

■ PASTA À LA WOODWARD

My friend Elizabeth Woodward, for whom this recipe is named, has for many hectic years held down important positions at Harvard University. Like many working women who entertain friends and colleagues at home, she is often faced with the question "What can I make that's delicious but easy and quick to prepare?" This recipe is her answer.

Ripe tomatoes fresh from the garden and fresh spinach produce a nutritious, savory, and beautiful dish.

Cook the pasta until *al dente*. Drain and transfer to a large heated serving bowl.

Quickly add the tomatoes, onion, and mushroom slices, and toss to mix. Add the pesto and toss to cover completely. Add the spinach and pine nuts and toss, continuing to work quickly so the pasta stays hot.

Taste and correct the seasoning with the salt and pepper. Serve on heated plates and pass the Parmesan cheese.

Serves 6

9 ounces fresh fettuccine or other pasta

4 large ripe tomatoes, peeled, seeded, and chopped coarsely

1 cup chopped red onion

1 cup sliced mushroom caps

3/4 cup pesto sauce (see p. 108) or to taste

5 ounces fresh spinach, washed, spun dry, tough stems removed and chopped coarsely

1/2 cup pine nuts

Salt and freshly ground black pepper

Freshly grated Parmesan cheese

■ PORTOBELLO PIZZA

1 small head of garlic

1 tablespoon olive oil

2–3 tablespoons dry white wine

¾ cup fresh Italian buffalo
    mozzarella, diced small

2 small tomatoes, peeled, seeded,
    and chopped small

¼ cup scallion, white only, thinly
    sliced

⅛ cup fresh basil, snipped with
    scissors

Salt and freshly ground black
    pepper

Butter, to grease baking dish

2 large portobello mushrooms,
    stems removed and caps
    brushed with a damp paper
    towel or piece of muslin

2 tablespoons coarsely grated
    fresh Parmesan cheese

This hearty dish is a closer relative to a designer pizza than to its very distant cousin, the "stuffed mushroom." It's a great way to use a couple of freshly pulled scallions, and it's perfect fare for a luncheon for two, served with a good crusty bread.

Preheat the oven to 450°F.

Slice the top off the garlic head, cutting through the tops of the cloves. Place it in a small roasting pan or terra-cotta garlic roaster and drizzle the oil over the top. Roast for 30 minutes and allow to cool.

Reduce the oven heat to 400°F.

Squeeze each roasted clove out of its peel into a small bowl and mash. Combine with the wine to produce a moist paste. Set aside.

In a second bowl, combine the mozzarella, tomatoes, scallion, basil, and salt and pepper to taste. Set aside.

Butter a baking dish large enough to hold the mushroom caps. Place the caps, gill side up, in the dish. Divide the garlic paste evenly between them and spread over the exposed surface. Pile the mozzarella mixture on top and sprinkle each cap with a tablespoon of grated Parmesan.

Bake for about 10 minutes or until the cheeses have melted.

Serves 2

■ TOMATOES FLORENTINE

I have always enjoyed making these stuffed tomatoes, in part because they're easy to prepare but mostly because they taste so good.

Sun-ripened tomatoes from my garden make this a very special dish. I serve them as appetizers, accompaniments for fish and meat, or as part of an antipasto platter, where they are almost always the first to go.

Cut each tomato in half horizontally. With a grapefruit spoon or melon baller, scoop out each half without squeezing the tomatoes or breaking through the skin. Sprinkle with salt. Invert on a rack and drain for at least 30 minutes. (The tomatoes can be prepared to this point earlier in the day.) Turn on the broiler.

Blanch the spinach leaves in boiling water for 3 seconds. Run them under cold water to stop the cooking. Drain and chop coarsely.

In a small skillet, heat 2 teaspoons of the olive oil. Add the shallot and sauté, stirring, until tender. Do not brown. Remove the skillet from the heat and add the spinach, stirring, to combine.

Combine the spinach mix, bread crumbs, and feta. Taste and correct the seasoning with salt and pepper. Fill each tomato half with the spinach mixture, sprinkle with Parmesan, and place each half on a broiler pan. Drizzle the tomatoes with the remaining olive oil and place them under the broiler (about 5 or so inches from the heat) for 3 to 4 minutes, or until the cheese turns golden brown. Do not let the cheese burn.

Serve immediately or at room temperature.

Serves 6

3 large firm, ripe tomatoes

Salt

1/3 cup young spinach leaves, washed and drained

1 tablespoon plus 2 teaspoons extra-virgin olive oil

1 large clove shallot, minced finely

1/3 cup crumbs from freshly grated stale French bread

1/3 cup crumbled feta cheese

Freshly ground black pepper

Freshly grated Parmesan cheese

■ NYUOM PENG PAH (Tomato Salad)

Salad

1½ large chicken breast

1½ pounds plum tomatoes, stem ends trimmed, very thinly sliced

1 large, seedless cucumber, or 3 pickling cucumbers, scored and thinly sliced

1 cup loosely packed fresh mint leaves

1 cup loosely packed fresh basil leaves, preferably Thai lemon basil

Thinly sliced bird's-eye or Tabasco chilis, to taste (available in Asian markets and many supermarkets)

Tuk Trey (Dressing)

½ cup granulated sugar

1 garlic clove

1 small shallot

5 teaspoons lime juice

½ cup fish sauce (available in Asian markets and many supermarkets)

2 teaspoons salt

Longteine De Monteiro is the charming Cambodian owner-chef who oversees three excellent restaurants in the Boston area. I first tasted this dish at her original restaurant, the Elephant Walk. You'll find it a luscious use of your sun-ripened tomatoes and so easy to prepare.

In a large saucepan, bring 4 cups water to a boil and add the chicken breast. Return the water to a boil, then lower the heat to simmer, cooking for 10 to 15 minutes or until the chicken is tender. Remove the chicken from the pot, allowing it to cool slightly, then shred the meat along the grain with your fingers.

In a large salad bowl, combine all of the salad ingredients and set aside.

To make the dressing, bring ¼ cup water to a boil in a small saucepan. Add the sugar and the salt, stirring to dissolve them. Set aside and allow to cool.

With a mortar and pestle, pound the garlic and shallot into small pieces or grind them in a mini-chopper. Stir the garlic-shallot paste into the sugar water, then add the remaining dressing ingredients.

To serve, add the dressing to the salad to taste. Toss and serve immediately. Do not allow the vegetables to get soggy.

Serves 6 to 8

Chapter 18
Mixed Vegetables

Cassoulet (p. 86)

These recipes call for a mixture of vegetables that will not all be ready to harvest at the same time. If you choose to follow the instructions exactly, you will need to supplement the vegetables from your garden with others from the market. Or you can substitute similar vegetables from your garden. Either way, you'll find the results quite tasty.

Roasting vegetables has become a popular way to prepare them. Wash, peel, and trim all the vegetables you plan to roast. Place them in a baking pan in one layer. Brush them with a little olive oil. Add approximately ¼ inch water and roast them in a 400°F pre-heated oven for 45 minutes to 1¼ hours. Check occasionally to make sure the water has not evaporated.

■ CASSOULET

1/4 pound thick-cut smoked bacon, sliced thinly

2 tablespoons extra-virgin olive oil

3 medium onions, chopped coarsely

3 cloves garlic, minced

3/4 pound lamb stew meat, cut into 1 1/2-inch cubes

4 cups coarsely chopped red Swiss chard

1 pound small white beans, soaked overnight in water to cover

1 low-fat kielbasa sausage, cut into 12 pieces

6 roasted chicken legs

3 medium ripe tomatoes, peeled and chopped coarsely

2 rounded teaspoons light brown sugar

Salt and freshly ground black pepper

1 tablespoon freshly squeezed lemon juice (optional)

Many years ago, on my first visit to the Languedoc in France, I was told of a legendary cassoulet that was put on the stove the day the German army surrendered in 1918 and was taken off the heat on the day the German army invaded France in 1940.

Our variation on this classic calls for roasted chicken in place of the traditional duck confit, low-fat sausages, and fresh vegetables from your garden.

In a heavy-bottomed stewpot or metal casserole, over medium-high heat, render the bacon until it begins to brown. Add the oil, onion, and garlic. Cook, stirring, until the vegetables are soft. Add the lamb and brown it all over. Add the Swiss chard and cook, stirring, until the vegetable wilts.

Drain the beans and add to the pot. Add the sausage, chicken legs, tomatoes, sugar, and just enough water to cover. Reduce the heat to medium-low, cover, and cook for 1 hour and 45 minutes. When the beans begin to soften, add the salt and pepper to taste. Cook for an additional 1 hour and 45 minutes or until the beans are very soft. Remove from heat. Pull the meat off the bones if necessary. Discard chicken bones.

If you like a tarter flavor, add the lemon juice just before serving.

Serves 6 to 8

■ MIXED VEGETABLE AND MEAT STEW WITH LEMON SAUCE

In Greece this stew is served at weekly family dinners. Home cooks prepare it early in the day, then take it to the local baker, who finishes it in his oven. The lemon sauce perfectly balances the flavor of celery.

Add whichever vegetables are crying to be picked in your garden.

In a large heavy-bottomed pot for which you have a cover, heat the oil and add the butter until it melts. Add the onions and sauté until soft but not brown. Add the celery and meat and sauté on high heat, stirring, until the meat and vegetables are brown, about 5 minutes.

Add the beans, potatoes, and any other vegetables you wish to add and season with the salt and pepper. Stir to mix. Add 2 to 3 cups boiling water just to cover.

Lower the heat and simmer 1½ hours, or until the meat is tender.

Turn the meat and vegetables out into a warm serving bowl and keep warm.

Beat the eggs about 3 minutes in an electric mixer or until thick and light yellow. Slowly add the lemon juice while beating. Beat ¼ cup hot stew liquid into the eggs. While beating, gradually add ¾ cup more hot stew liquid. Turn the sauce into a saucepan and cook, stirring, until the sauce begins to thicken.

Pour the sauce over the meat and vegetables and serve immediately with hot crusty bread if desired.

Serves 6 to 8

1 tablespoon olive oil

1 tablespoon unsalted butter

2 large onions, coarsely chopped

1 head celery, thick outer stalks removed, cut into 1-inch pieces

1½ pounds lean lamb stew meat, cut into 2-inch cubes

1 cup string beans, cut in half

3 medium red potatoes, cut into quarters

2 cups mixed vegetables from your garden

1 teaspoon kosher salt

Freshly ground black pepper

3 large eggs

Juice of 2 lemons

Crusty bread (optional)

■ COLD NOODLE SALAD

1 pound spaghetti, broken in two

¾ cup canola or sunflower seed
   oil

2 tablespoons toasted sesame oil

2 tablespoons sesame seeds

¾ cup soy sauce

Pinch of granulated sugar

6 scallions, trimmed white
   and 3 inches of green, sliced
   ¼ inch thick

12 sugar snap peas, strings
   removed and sliced in half
   diagonally

1 cup grated carrots

1 cup bean sprouts, refreshed in
   ice water and drained

*You can make this quick and easy, practically no-cook dish
several hours ahead and then chill it. It's especially good on a hot
summer day.*

Cook the spaghetti *al dente*. Do not allow it to get too
soft. Drain and set aside.

In the same pan, heat the oils. Add the sesame seeds and
cook, stirring, until they begin to brown. Remove from the
heat and stir in soy sauce and sugar. Add the spaghetti and
toss to coat. Add the vegetables and toss again to coat.

Refrigerate until cold, 4 or 5 hours.

Serves 8

■ FALL VEGETABLE TAGINE

This is one of my favorite dishes from the kitchen of Paul Sussman and Ellis Seidman, the two incredibly creative chef-owners of Daddy-O's Bohemian Cafe in Cambridge, Massachusetts.

Paul and Ellis are dedicated to the use of only the freshest seasonal vegetables. They are also active members of the Chefs' Collaborative, an organization devoted to the support of sustainable agriculture.

Melt the butter in a heavy pot. Add the onions and sauté over medium heat until lightly browned. Add seasonings and fennel and sauté 2 or 3 minutes.

Add 5 cups water, carrots, parsley, and cilantro, and bring to a boil. Reduce the heat and simmer for 15 minutes. Add turnips and butternut squash and simmer for an additional 15 minutes, adding more water if necessary. Add the zucchini and chickpeas and simmer 20 minutes longer. The consistency should be that of a thick soup. If too thin, bring to a boil and reduce.

Correct the seasoning and serve over couscous. Garnish with walnuts and raisins if desired.

Serves 6

4 ounces unsalted butter

2 cups diced onions

1/2 teaspoon minced fresh ginger

1/2 teaspoon ground ginger

1/4 teaspoon saffron threads

1/2 teaspoon ground coriander

1 teaspoon freshly ground black pepper

2 teaspoons salt

1/2 cup diced fennel bulb

1 1/2 cups sliced carrots

3 tablespoons chopped fresh parsley

3 tablespoons chopped fresh cilantro

1 1/2 cups medium-diced turnips

1 1/2 cups medium-diced butternut squash or other winter squash

1 1/2 cups sliced zucchini

1/2 cup chickpeas, soaked overnight and cooked until soft in salted water, 1 to 2 hours, or canned, washed, and drained

Toasted walnuts and raisins for garnish (optional)

■ FISHERMEN'S PIE

Marinade

1 clove garlic, minced

1 tablespoon freshly squeezed
    lemon juice

¼ teaspoon grated lemon rind

¼ teaspoon granulated sugar

⅛ teaspoon kosher salt

3 tablespoons extra-virgin olive oil

Vegetable Filling

1 roasted red bell pepper, cut into
    strips

¼ cup minced shallots

2 large leeks, white end plus 2 inches
    of green, washed thoroughly and
    cut into thin strips

1 cup baby carrots, quartered
    lengthwise, or young carrots,
    quartered lengthwise and then
    sliced horizontally into 2- to
    3-inch pieces

1 cup broccoli florets

¾ cup green beans, sliced into
    2-inch pieces

1 cup sugar snap peas, strings
    removed

Ingredients continue on p. 91

One of the joys of writing this cookbook has been the opportunity to experiment with the wonderful flavors that only garden-fresh and garden-ripe vegetables can offer. Because all the vegetables in this variation on the age-old traditional shepherd's pie won't be ripe at the same time, use as many of them as you have and buy the rest.

Preheat the oven to 400°F.

Make the marinade: In a large stainless-steel or glass bowl, combine all the ingredients except the olive oil and whisk until the sugar and salt are dissolved. While whisking, add the olive oil in a steady but slow stream.

Add all the Vegetable Filling ingredients to the bowl and toss to coat. Let sit at room temperature for 10 minutes. Soak the scallops in the milk for 5 minutes.

Meanwhile prepare the Béchamel Sauce: In a small saucepan, melt the butter. Whisk in the flour a bit at a time. While whisking continuously, slowly pour in the milk a little at a time. Make sure there are no lumps. Add the salt, pepper, and nutmeg and whisk until combined. Continue to cook, stirring, until the sauce is the consistency of thick cream. Set aside until needed, stirring occasionally to prevent a skin from forming.

Heat a seasoned or nonstick wok. Add the vegetables and marinade and stir-fry for 5 minutes. Add the shrimp and scallops and cook, stirring, until the shrimp begins to color and the scallops begin to become opaque. Add the imitation crabmeat and stir for 2 minutes longer.

Turn the seafood and vegetables into a 2-quart glass

or ceramic casserole. Stir the Béchamel Sauce and add to the casserole. Mix.

Drain and mash the potatoes. Add the 4 tablespoons melted butter and buttermilk and mix completely. Stir in the cheese, salt, and pepper. Set aside.

Stir the contents of the casserole one more time. Turn the mashed potatoes into the casserole and smooth the top. Dot with the butter cubes and bake for 30 minutes. If the potatoes have not begun to color, place the casserole under the broiler for 5 or so minutes until the potatoes begin to brown.

Serves 8

Seafood Filling

½ pound bay scallops

1 cup whole milk

½ pound medium shrimp, shelled, deveined, and tails removed

1 8-ounce package imitation crabmeat

Béchamel Sauce

2 tablespoons unsalted butter

2 tablespoons all-purpose flour

1 cup whole milk in which scallops were soaked

¼ teaspoon salt

5 grinds black pepper

Pinch of ground nutmeg

Mashed Potato Topping

4 large russet or other baking potatoes, peeled and boiled until very tender

4 tablespoons melted unsalted butter

¼ cup skim buttermilk at room temperature

¼ cup freshly grated Parmesan cheese

¾ teaspoon salt

5 grinds black pepper

1 tablespoon unsalted butter, cut into small cubes

■ GARDEN EGGS

6 sourdough English muffins,
   halves separated

4 tablespoons unsalted butter

2 tablespoons olive oil

3 small Yukon Gold or other waxy
   potatoes, boiled until just
   tender and cut into 1/2-inch
   dice

1 crookneck squash or zucchini,
   cut into fine matchsticks

3 scallions, trimmed, white and
   green, sliced into fine
   matchsticks

1 small red bell pepper, roasted,
   peeled, and cut into
   matchsticks

1/2 cup fresh English peas, shelled

1 large tomato, peeled, seeded,
   and chopped coarsely

1 teaspoon pimentón (Spanish
   smoked sweet pepper powder)
   or paprika

3/4 teaspoon kosher salt

12 large eggs, lightly beaten with

1 teaspoon chopped fresh thyme

Salt and freshly ground black
   pepper

Grated Pecorino Romano cheese

Sprigs of fresh thyme for garnish

Scrambled eggs are synonymous with breakfast, but this mix of savory vegetables makes the traditional comfort food something very special.

Serve these eggs with crisp bacon, little pork sausages, or additional sautéed vegetables.

With a 3-inch serrated cookie cutter, cut out the centers of the muffin tops. (Save the centers for some other use.) Melt 2 tablespoons butter and brush on the bottom and the remainder of the top and toast on a hot nonstick skillet or griddle. Put together and set aside.

In the same skillet, heat the oil. Add the potatoes and sauté until they begin to brown. Add the remaining vegetables except the tomatoes and sauté 3 minutes, stirring. Add the tomatoes and sprinkle the pimentón and salt over the vegetables and stir in. Cook 1 minute longer.

With a slotted spoon, remove the vegetables to a bowl and set aside.

Combine the eggs and thyme. Add the remaining 2 tablespoons butter to the skillet and heat until melted. Add the eggs and cook, stirring, until the eggs are at the soft stage. Correct the seasoning with salt and pepper to taste. Add the vegetables and toss gently for 1 minute, or until the eggs are the consistency you prefer. Do not overcook.

Place one reassembled toasted English muffin on each of 6 serving plates. Divide the scrambled eggs into the center and around each, sprinkle with grated cheese, and garnish with sprigs of fresh thyme.

Serve with bacon, sausages, or additional sautéed vegetables.

Serves 6

■ GLORIOUS GARBAGE RELISH

This recipe arose from the need to empty the refrigerator. It was time to make room for the next harvest, but how could I throw away any of my lovingly produced vegetables? Necessity, that proverbial mother of invention, came to the rescue.

I just kept chopping and adding and slicing and mixing until my largest stainless-steel bowl was full. The result was a spectacular array of color and fabulous taste that will bring garden flavor to your table throughout the year.

Fill a 4-quart or larger stainless-steel or glass mixing bowl with the vegetables and toss to mix. Sprinkle one-third of the salt over the vegetables and toss. Repeat this process with the remaining salt, cover, and refrigerate for 24 hours.

The following day, drain the liquid into a 6-quart pot. Set the vegetables aside.

To the liquid, add all vinegar, sugar, mustard, mustard seed, celery seed, turmeric, and ginger, and stir to mix. Bring the liquid to a boil, lower the heat, and simmer 2 minutes. Strain and retain the liquid.

Rinse the pot and the mixing spoon and return the pickling liquid to the pot. Add all the vegetables and the spice bag and mix. Bring to a boil, lower the heat slightly, and simmer for 10 minutes, stirring once after 5 minutes.

Discard the spice bag and place 2 cups of vegetables and some liquid in the bowl of a food processor fitted with a steel blade. Pulse four times and turn out into a bowl to cool. Repeat until all the vegetables have been processed. Transfer the relish to 1- or 2-cup containers, cover, and freeze.

Yields approximately 8 cups

½ Vidalia onion or other sweet onion, coarsely chopped

½ large red onion, coarsely chopped

1 orange bell pepper, seeded and chopped

1 yellow bell pepper, seeded and chopped

2 jalapeño peppers, stems removed, seeded, and diced very small (be sure to wear rubber gloves!)

1 leek, white only, washed thoroughly and sliced

1 small red cabbage, core removed and shredded

½ green cabbage, core removed and shredded

4 ripe tomatoes, coarsely chopped

1 cucumber, washed thoroughly, quartered lengthwise, then sliced

3 beets, peeled, diced, and blanched for 3 minutes

½ cup sea salt

3 cups white vinegar

1¼ cups granulated sugar

1 tablespoon Dijon mustard

1 tablespoon slightly crushed mustard seed

1 tablespoon celery seed

¾ teaspoon turmeric

½ teaspoon grated fresh ginger

1 tablespoon mixed pickling spices, tied in cheesecloth bag

■ GRILLED VEGETABLES AND TWO DIPS

Sour Cream and Chive Dip

3/4 cup sour cream

2 tablespoons chives, snipped
   with a scissors

1 teaspoon soy sauce

1 teaspoon Dijon mustard

1 teaspoon grated fresh ginger

Salt and freshly ground black
   pepper to taste

2 scallions

Goat Cheese Dip

5 ounces goat cheese

2 large slices red onion, chopped

1/4 cucumber, peeled and chopped

Freshly ground 5-pepper blend
   (red, green, white, Szechuan,
   and black peppercorns,
   purchased as a combination
   or mixed at home)

Ingredients continue on p. 95

Grilling used to be limited to meats and fish. But if you've tasted vegetables cooked over hot coals or under the heat of a broiler, you know they have earned their place on gourmets' tables. I've suggested a selection of vegetables and quantities. Add or subtract as your garden or desires dictate. And because they will not all be ripe at the same time, you may need to visit the produce section of your supermarket.

Preparing the dips the day before will allow their flavors to marry.

In a bowl, combine all the ingredients for the Sour Cream and Chive Dip, except the scallions, and mix well.

Trim one scallion, leaving about 2 inches of green. Slice it in half lengthwise, then make as many matchstick slices as you like. Place them in a bowl with ice water and reserve them until needed. They will curl slightly. Drain and use as garnish.

In a blender jar, combine all the ingredients for the Goat Cheese Dip, except the pepper, and purée. Transfer to a small serving bowl and garnish with the freshly grated pepper.

In a stainless-steel or glass bowl, combine all the marinade ingredients and whisk. Set aside, leaving the whisk in the bowl.

Dip each raw vegetable and mushroom in the marinade, whisking between dips, and place it in a large roasting pan. Cover the pan until you are ready to grill. The vegetables are best when the marinade is applied several hours ahead.

Grill each piece over hot coals or 2 inches from the heating element of a broiler until brown. Turn the vegetables and mushrooms frequently.

Watch them carefully because they brown at different rates. Some, like the asparagus, will take only 1 minute on each side. The total grilling time overall is about 15 minutes.

Serve with the dips.

Serves 8 to 10

Marinade

1 cup olive oil

Juice of ½ lemon

2 garlic cloves, finely minced

2 teaspoons salt

1 teaspoon freshly ground black pepper

1 sweet Italian pepper, seeded and cut into 8 long pieces

1 red bell pepper, seeded and cut into 6 long pieces

16 spears asparagus, bottoms trimmed and peeled halfway to the tip

6 scallions, trimmed and measuring about 5 inches (white and green combined)

2 yellow summer squash, ends trimmed and quartered vertically

2 small zucchini, ends trimmed and quartered vertically

12 medium portobello mushrooms, stems removed

Narrow end of 1 butternut squash, peeled and cut into ¼ inch slices

■ MEDITERRANEAN LAMB AND VEGETABLE STEW

2 jalapeño peppers

4 tablespoons extra-virgin olive oil

1½–2 pounds lamb stew meat

1 teaspoon pimentón (Spanish
    smoked sweet pepper powder)
    or paprika

1 teaspoon kosher salt

Freshly ground black pepper

4 green cardamom pods

2 tablespoons lemon juice mixed
    with 1 tablespoon water

3 carrots, trimmed, scraped,
    halved, and then cut into strips

3 medium turnips, trimmed,
    quartered from the top down,
    then cut into ½-inch strips

1 large onion, peeled, halved, and
    sliced

1 large ripe beefsteak tomato,
    peeled and coarsely chopped

2 medium zucchini, sliced ½-inch
    thick

1 cup golden raisins

Mediterranean cooking is characterized by its simplicity and robust flavors. This dish fills all the requirements and more. Its very slow cooking method retains the individual flavors of the ingredients and allows for lots of variation. Add whatever vegetables you have bursting to be picked that day and serve the stew over boiled rice, couscous, or buttered pasta.

Wearing rubber gloves, roast the jalapeño peppers until charred. Then stem, seed, and chop them, and set aside.

In a heavy-bottomed stew pan, heat the oil and add the meat. Brown the meat slowly all over, on a medium-low heat. Stir occasionally to keep it from burning.

Sprinkle with the pimentón and salt and stir to mix completely. Stir in the black pepper, cardamom, and lemon juice and water. Add the carrots and turnips and cover. Simmer for 1 hour, stirring occasionally, to make sure it is not burning. If necessary, add a little water.

Add the remaining ingredients and simmer, covered, for an additional 30 minutes. The meat should be tender, and the vegetables, having given up their liquid, will have produced a sauce.

Serves 6 to 8

■ ROASTED VEGETABLE TOWERS

This luscious tower calls for a combination of some of the sweetest herbs and vegetables from our gardens and markets. It's as beautiful as it is delicious.

Preheat the oven to 450°F.

Brush 2 large nonstick baking sheets liberally with olive oil. Place as many vegetable slices as possible in a single layer on each one and brush them liberally with olive oil too. Place the baking sheets on the bottom and middle shelves of the oven and bake the vegetables for about 10 minutes or until just tender. Remove the vegetable slices and set aside in one layer while you roast the remaining vegetables. Set aside.

Combine the Gorgonzola and goat cheeses and mix completely. Add the salt and pepper to taste (underestimate the salt because sea salt does not dissolve quickly) and chopped thyme. Combine and set aside.

On a nonstick, lightly oiled baking sheet, place 6 slices eggplant. Spread approximately 1 tablespoon cheese mixture on each slice. Cover the cheese with 2 slices potato, then 2 slices zucchini, 1 quartered bell pepper, and 1 slice onion. Cover the onion with 1 slice mozzarella, 1 slice tomato, and 2 more slices zucchini. Divide the remaining cheese mix over the zucchini and top with the remaining eggplant slices.

Using an oiled metal or wooden skewer, make a hole through the center of each tower and bake until the mozzarella has melted, about 5 or 6 minutes. Insert 1 sprig of thyme or rosemary into each hole and serve.

Serves 6

$1/3$–$1/2$ cup dark green, fragrant extra-virgin olive oil, plus more for brushing the baking sheets

2 white round eggplants, or the fattest part of 2 large purple eggplants, cut horizontally into 12 $1/3$-inch-thick slices

4 red potatoes, cut lengthwise into 12 thin slices

2 medium deep green zucchini, cut into 24 diagonal $1/4$-inch-thick slices

3 large plum tomatoes, cut lengthwise into 6 $1/3$-inch slices

1 large red onion, peeled and cut horizontally into 6 $1/4$-inch slices

$1\frac{1}{2}$ red bell peppers, stems and membranes removed, seeded and quartered

$1/4$ cup imported Gorgonzola cheese mixed with

4 ounces goat cheese

6 $1/4$-inch-thick slices mozzarella cheese

Sea salt and freshly ground black pepper

2 teaspoons chopped fresh lemon thyme

6 sprigs fresh lemon thyme or rosemary, lower leaves only removed

■ PRICKLY VEGETABLE TEMPURA

Dipping Sauce

1 tablespoon hon dashi
   (Japanese fish powder,
   available in Asian markets
   and many supermarkets)

¼ cup tamari

¼ cup mirin (Japanese sweet
   rice cooking wine)

1 tablespoon whiskey (optional)

Vegetables

1 medium sweet potato, peeled
   and sliced ½ inch thick on
   the diagonal

1 red bell pepper, stemmed,
   seeded, and cut into ½-inch
   strips

12 string beans or haricots verts,
   stems removed

1 large zucchini, sliced on the
   diagonal into 8 ½-inch-thick
   pieces

4 spears asparagus, root end
   trimmed

8 tender inner stalks of celery
   with leaves, root ends trimmed

1 medium carrot, about 7 inches
   long, ends trimmed, peeled,
   halved, and then cut into
   eighths lengthwise

2 medium green tomatoes, each
   cut in 4 slices

Ingredients continue on p. 99

We all think of tempura as quintessentially Japanese, yet the Portuguese probably introduced it to Japan in the sixteenth century. Before the arrival of Europeans, Japanese food was either steamed or boiled, as some of the best food there still is.

This adventure in cross-cultural cuisine is made even more alluring by the introduction of Chinese bean threads. Most of the vegetables called for in this recipe are available for harvest in late summer or early fall, but any combination of firm vegetables, any time of the year, can be dipped in tempura batter and deep-fried.

Combine all the Dipping Sauce ingredients with 3 tablespoons water in a small saucepan and taste. Add more water, 1 tablespoon at a time, if you find the sauce too salty. Bring it to a boil, remove it from the heat immediately, and allow it to cool. Set aside.

Place the sweet potato in a steamer, cover, and steam until just tender, not soft. Add the pepper, beans, zucchini, and asparagus and steam, covered, 1 minute. Remove all the vegetables to paper towels, pat dry, and allow to cool to room temperature. (There is no need to steam the celery, carrot, or tomatoes.)

When ready to serve, prepare the batter.

Follow the package directions. Be sure to use ice water in making the batter. The colder the batter, the quicker it will puff up.

Pour oil into a wok or deep fryer to a depth of about 2½ inches and heat. The oil has reached the correct temperature when a bit of batter dropped in it falls halfway to the bottom and rises immediately to the top. Strain all excess batter from the oil.

Dip the vegetables one at a time into the batter, then roll them in the noodle pieces and gently put them in the oil.

Put in as many as the wok will accommodate without them sticking. The vegetables will float to the top when they are cooked. They should be crisp and beginning to brown. Remove each piece to paper towels and keep warm. Repeat the process until all the vegetables are fried.

You can garnish the plate, if desired, with deep-fried kale leaves (stems removed), parsley, or other leafy herbs or vegetables. Do not dip the garnish in batter.

Serve immediately. Pass the Dipping Sauce or serve it in individual dipping bowls.

Serves 4

Batter

1 package tempura batter mix (available in Asian markets and many supermarkets)

1 cup bean thread noodles, softened in hot water, dried, and cut into small pieces (available in Asian markets and many supermarkets)

Corn oil for deep-frying

Kale leaves, parsley, or other leafy vegetable or herb, for garnish (optional)

■ JAPANESE RICE AND VEGETABLES

1½ teaspoons hon dashi (Japanese fish powder, available in Asian markets and many supermarkets)

2 tablespoons dark soy sauce

2 tablespoons sake or rice wine

1 teaspoon salt

1 tablespoon fresh ginger, cut into thin slivers

1 small boned and skinned chicken breast, cut into thin strips

2½ cups Japanese or short-grain rice

Vegetables, such as carrots, green peppers, red peppers, haricots verts, string beans, sugar snap peas, cut into bite-sized pieces

1 egg per serving

The Japanese often serve this dish as a main course, very hot and heaped in a bowl. Chefs break an egg over the top and cover each bowl. The steam from the rice cooks the protein-rich egg.

Use as many different vegetables as your garden will supply. And roasting them over coals for a short time will impart a unique flavor to the rice.

Combine all the ingredients, except the rice, vegetables, and eggs, with 4 cups boiling water, and stir until the salt is dissolved.

Wash the rice in 2 changes of water, strain, and put into a rice cooker with the "boiling liquid." Add the chicken and cook.

If you do not have a rice cooker, choose a heavy-bottomed pot for which you have a tight-fitting lid. Put the rice and chicken in the pot and pour the liquid over it, cover, and bring to boil over medium-high heat. Raise the heat to high and cook until the liquid is almost completely absorbed. Reduce the heat to low and add the vegetables. Cover and continue cooking until all the liquid is absorbed, 7 to 10 minutes.

Uncover and spread a clean tea towel over the pot. Place the cover over the towel and let stand for 10 minutes before serving. The towel will keep the heat in to allow the rice to continue to cook but will absorb any condensation.

To serve, fill individual bowls with the rice, break one egg over the rice in each bowl, and cover tightly with aluminum foil, until the egg is steamed.

Serves 8 to 10

CHAPTER 19
HERBS

Most gardeners reserve a section of their garden for culinary herbs that impart a touch of fragrance to every dish. An herb garden need not take up a great deal of room and can still accommodate a large number of these aromatic plants.

A basic kitchen garden will include parsley, which was used by the ancient Greeks and Romans both for its taste and its professed medicinal qualities. I'm not sure it cures anything, but chewing it after consuming raw onions certainly has a salutary effect on the breath. Cilantro, the fresh leaves of the herb coriander, is a happy addition to Mexican, Middle Eastern, and Indian dishes. If you want to dress up a simple piece of fish, sprinkle some freshly chopped tarragon on it. Rosemary is a native of the Mediterranean, and it is particularly good with poultry, lamb, and other meats. Crushed, it gives off a powerful fragrance that is mirrored in its taste. Savory also comes from the Mediterranean. The Romans mixed it with vinegar or sour verjuice to use as a sauce for almost everything. And basil, though it probably originated in India and still has some religious significance there, is more often associated with Italian cuisine. Thyme, oregano, and marjoram are other widely used culinary herbs.

While it's possible to use and obtain dried herbs, fresh herbs are much tastier.

■ SCARBOROUGH FAIR HERB RUB

1½ cups fresh Italian parsley leaves

2 tablespoons fresh sage (about 12 leaves)

2 tablespoons fresh rosemary

2 tablespoons fresh thyme

8 cloves garlic, peeled

½ cup extra-virgin olive oil

This seasoning of fresh flavors for chicken, fish, and even some vegetables was inspired by the classic Simon and Garfunkel song. All these herbs will be fully mature at the same time, so you'll find it a simple matter of gathering what you need from your kitchen herb garden. It's truly a melodious marriage of fresh flavors.

Place the herbs and garlic in the bowl of a food processor fitted with a steel blade. Pulse to chop. While processing, slowly pour the oil in until blended.

For roasting or baking chicken: Spread 1 tablespoon of herb rub per pound of chicken all over bird and allow it to stand in the refrigerator overnight.

For fish: Spread 1 tablespoon per pound of fish. Refrigerate 1 hour, then poach, broil, or grill.

For vegetables: Stir well and drizzle 1 tablespoon of herb rub per pound of vegetables to be roasted.

The herb rub will keep for 2 to 3 weeks, refrigerated, in a tightly closed jar.

Yields about ⅔ cup

■ FRUTCH'S BASIL-LEMON CHICKEN

Chicken broth, or water, to cover
chicken

2 boneless, skinless chicken
breasts

1 orange bell pepper, trimmed,
seeded, and chopped small

1 yellow bell pepper, trimmed,
seeded, and chopped small

3 scallions, trimmed, white and
2 inches of green, sliced fine

3/4 cup basil leaves, snipped small
with a scissors

Rind of 1 large lemon, coarsely
grated

Juice of 1 large lemon

3 tablespoons honey

1 tablespoon freshly ground
five-pepper blend or black
pepper

1 teaspoon salt

1/2 cup olive oil

Whole basil leaves or lettuce
leaves for garnish

Basil, like tomatoes and zucchini, is a crop that grows in abundance every summer. This aromatic chicken salad is my next-door neighbor's answer to her bounty. It's an easy recipe to double.

Bring the broth or water to a slow boil and poach the chicken breasts until done, about 20 minutes. Cool and cut into 1/2-inch cubes. Transfer the chicken to a bowl and add the peppers and scallions. Refrigerate.

In a nonreactive bowl, combine the remaining ingredients, except the oil and basil leaves. Slowly add the oil, whisking, to incorporate completely. Pour over the chicken and return to the refrigerator to chill.

When ready to serve, prepare a ring of large basil leaves or lettuce leaves on each of 4 plates. With a slotted spoon, divide the chilled salad into the center of the basil rings, drizzle a little of the dressing on the leaves, and serve.

Serves 4

■ HERBED FRUIT AND CORNMEAL STUFFING FOR PEPPERS AND MORE

The marriage of savory fresh herbs, dried fruit, and vegetables picked fresh from your garden will make this a truly memorable stuffing. Stuff other vegetables or poultry or bake it separately.

Preheat the oven to 400°F.

Soak the apricots in warm water to cover and set aside.

Combine the melted butter, onions, carrots, and garlic in a skillet and sauté, stirring occasionally, until the onions are golden brown, about 12 to 15 minutes.

Drain the apricots and cut them into strips or chop coarsely.

In a large bowl, combine all the ingredients, except the bell peppers, and toss to mix.

Slice off the tops of the bell peppers, if using, and remove the seeds. Blanch them with boiling water 1 minute. Remove the peppers to cold water to stop the cooking, drain, and dry. Fill the peppers with the stuffing until they mound slightly. Place them in a buttered baking dish, add ¼ cup water, and bake for 30 minutes or until a toothpick inserted into the stuffing comes out clean.

Or, butter a baking pan and turn the stuffing into it.

Bake for 40 minutes or until the edges have pulled away from the sides and are well browned.

Or, fill a bird's cavity loosely with the stuffing, sew or skewer the cavity closed, and roast according to instructions for the bird.

Yields about 4 to 5 cups

8 ounces dried apricots

3 tablespoons unsalted butter, melted, plus more for buttering the dish

1 cup chopped onions

1 cup shredded carrots

5 cloves garlic, peeled and chopped fine

1 cup pine nuts

3 cups corn bread crumbs

¼ cup chopped fresh Italian (flat-leaf) parsley

2 tablespoons fresh thyme leaves or 1 tablespoon dried

1 tablespoon chopped fresh sage

1 large sweet-tart green apple, such as Mutsu

½ cup rich chicken broth

2 large eggs, lightly beaten

¼ teaspoon salt

¼ teaspoon freshly ground black pepper

6 red or yellow bell peppers (optional)

■ HERBED GNOCCHI

2 large baking potatoes, peeled
and quartered

Kosher salt for boiling water

2 large eggs, separated

1 teaspoon salt

1 teaspoon finely chopped fresh
thyme, plus more for garnish

1 teaspoon finely chopped fresh
oregano, plus more for garnish

1 teaspoon finely chopped fresh
chives, plus more for garnish

2 tablespoons light cream

1 cup semolina flour (available in
Italian markets and many
supermarkets)

Sauce

4 pieces thickly sliced sugar-cured
bacon, chopped

2 tablespoons unsalted butter

2 tablespoons all-purpose flour

1/2 cup heavy cream

1/2 cup milk

3 tablespoons freshly grated
Parmesan cheese, plus more for
passing (optional)

Salt and freshly ground black
pepper

*Herb gardens are the inspiration for this tasty dish. The flavor
and presentation of the finished gnocchi are further enhanced
by garnishing them with additional snippets of the herbs called
for and any others you may wish to use. I add lavender flowers,
chervil, tarragon, or any other aromatic herbs that I have
growing in my garden.*

Boil the potatoes in salted water until very soft. Remove
the pot from the stove and let them cool in the water.

Start a large pot of water boiling. Add 1 level teaspoon
salt for every quart of water in the pot.

Beat the egg whites until they form soft peaks. Set aside.

In a large bowl, combine the 1 teaspoon salt and
1 teaspoon of each of the herbs. Set aside.

Drain the potatoes and return them to the pot. Add
the light cream and the egg yolks and beat all together.
The potatoes should be wet.

Carefully measure 2 cups of the beaten potatoes and
add to the herbs. Beat to combine thoroughly. Beat in the
egg whites and then fold in the semolina. Your dough will
be wet.

When the water is boiling furiously, drop in the batter,
1 teaspoon at a time. Do not boil more than 8 gnocchi at
once. When they rise, cook 2 minutes longer. With a slotted
spoon remove them to a surface covered with several layers of
paper towel. The gnocchi will begin to harden as they cool.

Skim bits of batter off the top of the water so that it will
begin to boil again. Repeat the process until you've used all
the batter.

In a large skillet, render the bacon until crisp. With a
slotted spoon, remove the bacon to a small bowl and set
aside.

Set the skillet and rendered bacon grease aside.

In a small pan, over low heat, melt the butter and whisk in the flour until completely mixed. While stirring, add the heavy cream and the milk and cook until the sauce begins to thicken. Still stirring, add the 3 tablespoons cheese and salt and pepper to taste. Turn off the heat.

Return the skillet to the stove and reheat the bacon grease. Add the gnocchi and reheat. Do not let them brown. Add the sauce and toss to cover.

If the skillet is attractive enough to take to the table, sprinkle the gnocchi with the crumbled bacon, garnish with additional chopped herbs, and serve.

If you wish to make a more formal presentation, turn the sauced gnocchi out on a serving platter and sprinkle with the bacon and herb garnish. Serve.

Pass additional cheese if desired.

Serves 6 as a first course or 4 as a main course

■ MY FAVORITE PESTO

4 cups loosely packed, washed, and dried basil leaves

3 cloves garlic, peeled and chopped

2 anchovy fillets, drained and chopped

¾ cup extra-virgin Spanish olive oil

½ cup pine nuts

½ cup plus 2 tablespoons freshly grated Parmesan cheese

Salt

Most of us who grow basil in our gardens end up with more than we can use before it flowers. This pesto sauce, redolent of the flavors of the Mediterranean, is an easy and delicious way to save your bountiful harvest and taste it year-round. The recipe calls for Spanish olive oil, but you can use any other extra-virgin olive oil. I prefer Spanish olive oil because of its light, subtle flavor.

You can freeze the pesto in glass or plastic containers. To freeze it in small amounts, place one or two tablespoons in ice cube trays and freeze, then put in small plastic freezer bags and seal. If your recipe calls for the pesto to be added in cooking, defrosting is not necessary. Otherwise, defrost it at room temperature.

Loosely pack the basil leaves, garlic, and anchovies in a blender container and add ¼ cup of the olive oil. Process until almost liquefied. Add the pine nuts, half of the cheese, and the remaining olive oil. Process until everything is completely liquefied. Mix in the remaining cheese, taste, and add salt as necessary. Pack in glass or plastic containers and refrigerate. You can freeze this pesto for up to a year. Defrost at room temperature.

Yields approximately 2 cups

CHAPTER 20
SEASONING MIXES

Make up a small supply of these spice mixes and keep them on hand to add splendid flavors to simply sautéed or blanched vegetables. Although commercial substitutes for these mixes are available, they are much more flavorful when made in small quantities at home.

■ GARAM MASALA

In northern India, this mixture of highly aromatic roasted spices is popular. It is often sprinkled over dishes just before serving but can be used late in the cooking process as well.

All Indian food stores and some supermarkets sell commercially prepared garam masala, but this recipe will ensure that you always have a fresh batch on hand.

1 teaspoon ground cinnamon

1/2 teaspoon ground cloves

1/4 teaspoon ground cardamom

1/4 teaspoon ground cumin

1/4 teaspoon ground coriander

Combine all the ingredients and mix thoroughly. Store in an airtight container.

■ REDUCED BALSAMIC VINEGAR

½ cup balsamic vinegar

Generous pinch of granulated
  sugar

*This reduction is a great substitute for concentrated pomegranate
juice, but it is also delicious on berries or in fruit salads.*

Combine the vinegar and the sugar in a small stainless-steel
or enameled saucepan. Stir until the sugar is completely
dissolved.

Bring the vinegar to a boil and cook on medium-high heat
until it begins to thicken, about 4 to 6 minutes.

Remove from the heat and cool. Place in containers and
cover tightly. Do not refrigerate.

Yields about ⅓ cup

■ SPICY SEASONING MIX

1 tablespoon white peppercorns

1 tablespoon black peppercorns

1 tablespoon green peppercorns

1 tablespoon Szechuan
  peppercorns

1 tablespoon whole coriander
  seeds

½ tablespoon allspice

*This mix can be used as you would use pepper. It is delicious
with eggs and wonderful on steamed and buttered vegetables.*

Place all the spices into a heavy plastic bag, press out all the
air, and tie or close it. Smash the spices with a hammer or
tenderizing mallet until what you have looks like a medium
grind of pepper. Shake the bag to mix thoroughly.

Pour the spices into a jar with a tight cover and keep it in
a cool dark place until needed.

ON KEEPING

This book makes no attempt to teach you how to can or preserve the surplus products from the garden. The conventional way of preserving is to cook the vegetables or fruits and then "put them up" in sterilized jars and inflict a "water bath" on the filled and, one hopes, properly sealed jars. This process consists of boiling the produce, jars and all, for some specified period of time.

It is a labor-intensive, time-consuming job that is often successful but occasionally is not. It is the occasional failures that concern me. It can be quite dangerous to eat food that has not been properly preserved, and for that reason I prefer to freeze.

Freezing is easy and fast. It does not destroy color, flavor, or nutrients and can be used as a method of preservation for most foods. But, perhaps most important, it is safe and convenient.

Some foods are not suited to freezing. You wouldn't freeze lettuce, for instance. On the other hand, you would not can it either. Some foods just have to be eaten fresh from the garden, thank goodness!

Here are some general rules for freezing *vegetables* and *fruits*.

1. Always choose items that are at the peak of their flavor and condition. Don't freeze bruised or decaying fruits or vegetables. Cut out bruised portions.

2. Wash everything, except berries, as if you were preparing them for dinner that night. Do not wash berries before freezing them. Rather, freeze berries on a cookie tray as soon after picking as possible. Then pack them in small quantities in plastic containers or freezer bags.

3. Blanch all other produce quickly with or in boiling water and immediately immerse it in ice water to stop the cooking process. Tomatoes and fruits such as peaches and apricots benefit by having their skins removed, and blanching makes them easy to peel.

4. Dry the produce thoroughly and place it in bags. Press as much air as possible from the bags and then seal them. Remember that produce must be cold so that no condensation takes place. Also, the more air in the bag, the more natural condensation will take place. Condensation then forms ice crystals and causes freezer burn.

5. Label your packages clearly, and be sure to mark them with the date.

6. One final warning. Defrost your frozen produce in the refrigerator or in a microwave. Once you have defrosted anything, animal or vegetable, do not refreeze it, for you may be refreezing bacteria-laden food. Contrary to conventional wisdom, freezing does not kill bacteria. In addition, refreezing considerably alters the taste of the food, and not for the good.

   Other methods of keeping bountiful harvests are by making chutneys or salsas or relishes and then packaging them in convenient quantities for freezing. Make and freeze tomato sauces or oven-dry tomatoes.

   You will find recipes throughout the book for foods that can be preserved this way.

Herbs — There is, of course, no substitute for fresh herbs in cooking, but if you cannot "winter" your herb garden by bringing it indoors, dry the herbs before the first frost. It is easy to dry herbs if you have a dry place in which to hang them. Tie smallish bundles of individual herbs and hang them upside down. When the leaves are very dry, put the leaves only into jars with tight-fitting covers and keep them in a dark cupboard when you are not using them.

   You can freeze dill, parsley, chives, and basil. Chop the herbs finely in a food processor or snip them with a scissors and put them in a plastic freezer bag. Press as much air out of the bag as possible and seal it with twist ties. Place it in the freezer. Dip into the bag whenever you need herbs for cooking.

   The flavor of fresh herbs can be imparted to vinegars and olive oil by immersing several stems of the herb in them. Remember to remove the remains of the herb once the medium has been flavored. Tarragon and rosemary work very well. You can use the flavored vinegar or oil to season fish or meat.

INGREDIENTS AND SUBSTITUTIONS

As you look through this book, some ingredients may not be familiar. These pages will help you find them or substitute more familiar or more easily obtained ingredients. In addition they will explain some techniques and shortcuts.

Bean thread noodles — Chinese clear dry noodles made from rice can be purchased in almost all supermarkets and in all Asian food stores.

Black vinegar — A Chinese rice-fermented vinegar that can be obtained in stores selling Asian foods. Nina Simonds, an expert on Asian cuisine, thinks that Chin Kiang is the best available in the United States. Substitute half the amount of Worcestershire sauce when black vinegar is not available.

Curry paste — An Indian paste made of canola oil, curry spices, chili, ginger, garlic, tamarind, ground lentils, salt, pepper, sugar, and acetic acid. It comes in three degrees of spiciness, hot, medium, and mild. It can be found in many supermarkets and in Indian food stores. Substitute curry powder mixed with a bit of oil.

Firik — A form of unripened wheat, it can be found in stores selling Middle Eastern products. Substitute long-grain brown rice, which may result in a slightly blander dish.

Garam masala — A sweet spice mixture that is often added to Indian dishes, it can be purchased in many supermarkets or Indian food stores. Substitute your own homemade mix (see p. 109).

Grapeseed oil — Oil pressed from the grape seeds, it has a slightly nutty flavor. You can find it in most gourmet food stores. Substitute canola or safflower oil.

Hon dashi — A Japanese soup-base powder made with dried bonita. It can be purchased in many supermarkets and all stores selling Asian food. Substitute chicken bouillon with a tiny drop of anchovy paste.

Kosher salt — A coarse-grained salt. It is used to "kosher" meats according to the laws of koshering by the Orthodox Jewish community and is used in many gourmet recipes because it dissolves more slowly than granulated salt. In some dishes this is preferable. This salt is available in most supermarkets. Substitute granulated, iodized salt.

Maggi — A bottled Swiss seasoning sauce that can be purchased in supermarkets. Substitute Worcestershire sauce.

Mirin — A Japanese sweet-rice cooking wine that can be purchased in most supermarkets and in stores selling Asian food. Substitute sherry or whiskey.

Orange lentils — It's been my experience that these lentils, which are often found in Indian dishes, cook a bit more quickly than brown or green lentils. They produce dishes that retain the golden color of the lentil. These lentils can be found in many supermarkets, in some Asian food stores, and in stores that specialize in Indian food. Substitute any color lentil for this one, but be prepared for a different color in the finished dish.

Orange blossom water and rosewater — Flower-petal-flavored water, available in Middle Eastern stores and some supermarkets. Substitute orange liqueur mixed with water. It will impart the flavor of oranges and not orange blossoms, but it will do the trick.

Pimentón — Ground dried red pimiento peppers that comes from Extremadura in Spain. It has a subtle smoky sweet pepper flavor. It can be purchased in some supermarkets, most gourmet food stores, and stores specializing in Spanish and Hispanic foods. Substitute with sweet Hungarian paprika, though it will not have the smoky element.

Pomegranate juice — The concentrated juice of the pomegranate is tart and fruity. Sometimes called pomegranate molasses, it can be obtained in many supermarkets and in most Middle Eastern food stores. Substitute Reduced Balsamic Vinegar (see p. 110).

Saffron — The orange dried stigma from a small purple crocus can be purchased in the spice section of most supermarkets.

Sambal badjak — Fresh ripe chili paste with onions. It is originally a product of Indonesia but is now made in the United States. It can be purchased in most supermarkets and in stores selling Asian products. Substitute any chili paste cooked with minced onions.

Sea salt — This is a very coarse-grained crystallized salt that is often made from the highly saline waters of the Mediterranean Sea. It is air- and sun-dried, then washed and dried again. This method produces large crystals of salt, which are usually offered in mills like pepper mills. The crystals dissolve even more slowly than kosher salt crystals and are particularly good if sprinkled on roasting vegetables. Purchase it in gourmet shops and some supermarkets. Substitute kosher salt.

Tempura batter — Packaged batter mix usually made in Japan. Purchase it in many supermarkets and all Asian food stores.

Vidalia onion — The true Vidalia is grown in the state of Georgia, though farmers in California are also trying to cultivate it. The Vidalia is a sweet onion that does not have the bite of other onions. It does not irritate the eyes or mucous membranes when you cut it. It has become very popular and is usually available in early spring in all supermarkets. Substitute a Spanish or Walla Walla onion, and add a pinch of sugar when sautéing.

ACKNOWLEDGMENTS

My late husband, Harvey Leibenstein, used to say that writing a cookbook had at least one great advantage over writing books on economics: the author had the proof of its utility immediately. The proof is on the tip of the tongue. In fact, it has taken many tongues and innumerable taste buds to ensure that this book will be used with joy and satisfaction.

No cookbook is ever produced by a single person, and I am indebted to a great many people for their help. Foremost I want to thank my assistants, Kathy Wheeler and Christina Le Fevre, for their hard, unswerving efforts in the kitchen. They tested and consulted with me on every recipe, often finding errors, omissions, or inconsistencies that I had overlooked in my effort to develop new and tasty dishes. They were as committed to this book as I am and contributed recipes, which bear their names.

Testing in the kitchen, however, is only the first step in determining whether a recipe is good. I considered a dish for inclusion in this cookbook only when nonprofessionals had seen, tasted, and given their approval. I am fortunate in having a discerning group of friends, family, and colleagues who were willing to taste-test and give their honest opinions.

I want to thank Nancy and Robert Dorfman; Jennifer and Edward Ford and their children, William and Susannah; Renee Haferkamp; Diane and Zvi Griliches; Geraldine and David Kaye; Joan and Arthur Kleinman; Pauline and Charles Maier; Joanne and James Moore; Susan and Leo Poverman; and Elizabeth and Robert Shenton for their willingness to taste discriminatingly and comment on various dishes. Their responses and suggestions were invaluable and gratifying.

My cousins in Mexico City, Julieta and Zelma Libnic and Gloria Kreimerman, were extremely helpful in obtaining or reconstructing dishes we had all enjoyed as children. Gloria's cook, Felipa Hernández, and my former nanny, Mercedes, were, as always, indispensable.

Without the kind sharing of recipes by my fellow food professionals, Longtiene De Monteiro, Bob Sargent, Paul Sussman and Ellis Seidman, Nina Simonds, and Ana Sortun, this book would have been much the poorer. I would also like to thank my colleagues in the Culinary Historians of Boston and the International Association of Cooking Professionals for their help and support.

My good friends, my agent Anne Edelstein, and my editor Frances Tenenbaum, deserve much of the credit for bringing this book to fruition.

Finally, I must thank a very dear friend, Diego Hidalgo, whose own authorial efforts, though in a field far removed from the culinary arts, were an inspiration to me. I am greatly indebted to him for his unyielding and unselfish support and encouragement.

It goes without saying that while this book could not have been completed without the help of the people I have just mentioned, I and I alone bear the responsibility for any errors in the text or in the recipes themselves.

– Margaret Leibenstein
Cambridge, Massachusetts
2000

Photo Credits

David Cavagnaro: iii, vi, 4, 7, 19, 21, 29, 33, 40, 45, 52, 59, 64, 69, 79, 88, 99, 103

Rick Mastelli: 13, 55, 73, 85, 95

Deborah Fillion: 117

INDEX

Titles available in the Taylor's Weekend Gardening Guides series:

Organic Pest and Disease Control
Safe and Easy Lawn Care
Window Boxes
Attracting Birds and Butterflies
Water Gardens
Easy, Practical Pruning
The Winter Garden
Backyard Building Projects
Indoor Gardens
Plants for Problem Places
Soil and Composting
Kitchen Gardens
Garden Paths
Easy Plant Propagation
Small Gardens
Topiaries & Espaliers
Fragrant Gardens
Cold Climate Gardening
The Cutting Garden
Cooking from the Garden

At your bookstore or by calling 1-800-225-3362